First World War
and Army of Occupation
War Diary
France, Belgium and Germany

29 DIVISION
Headquarters, Branches and Services
Royal Army Veterinary Corps
Assistant Director Veterinary Services
2 March 1916 - 31 October 1919

WO95/2290/3

The Naval & Military Press Ltd
www.nmarchive.com
Published in association with The National Archives

Published by

The Naval & Military Press Ltd

Unit 10 Ridgewood Industrial Park,

Uckfield, East Sussex,

TN22 5QE England

Tel: +44 (0) 1825 749494

www.naval-military-press.com

www.nmarchive.com

This diary has been reprinted in facsimile from the original. Any imperfections are inevitably reproduced and the quality may fall short of modern type and cartographic standards.

© **Crown Copyright**
Images reproduced by permission of The National Archives, London, England, 2015.

Contents

Document type	Place/Title	Date From	Date To
Heading	WO95/2290/3 Assistant Director Veterinary Services 1916 Mar-1919 Oct		
Heading	29th Division Divl Troops Asst Dir. Vety Service Mar 1916-Oct 1919		
War Diary	Suez Camp	02/03/1916	13/03/1916
War Diary	Port Said	14/03/1916	14/03/1916
War Diary	At Sea	15/03/1916	16/03/1916
War Diary	Marseilles	20/03/1916	20/03/1916
War Diary	Paris	21/03/1916	21/03/1916
War Diary	Long	22/03/1916	31/03/1916
War Diary	Blanquesal	01/04/1916	03/04/1916
War Diary	Acheux	04/04/1916	30/05/1916
Heading	War Diary of Major J.J Griffith A.V.S. A.D.V.S. 29th Division From 1st June 1916 To 30th June 1916		
War Diary	Acheux	01/06/1916	30/06/1916
Heading	War Diary of A.D.V.S 29th Division From 1st To 31st July 1916 Volume		
Miscellaneous	A.D.V.S. 29th Division	08/08/1916	08/08/1916
Miscellaneous	D.A.A. Q.M.G.	14/08/1916	14/08/1916
War Diary	Acheux	01/07/1916	25/07/1916
War Diary	Beauval	26/07/1916	30/07/1916
Heading	War Diary of A.D.V.S 29th Division From 1st August 1916 To 31st August 1916 Volume 6		
War Diary	Poperinghe	01/08/1916	31/08/1916
Heading	War Diary of Major J.J Griffith AVC A.D.V.S. 29th Division From 1st Sept 1916 To 30th Sept 1916 Volume 3		
War Diary	Poperinghe	01/09/1916	30/09/1916
Heading	War Diary of Major J.J Griffith AVC A.D.V.S. 29th Division From 1st October 1916 To 31st October 1916 Volume 8		
War Diary	Poperinghe (L'Ebbe Farm)	01/10/1916	06/10/1916
War Diary	Poperinghe	07/10/1916	07/10/1916
War Diary	Corbie	08/10/1916	09/10/1916
War Diary	Ribemont	11/10/1916	17/10/1916
War Diary	E 11 Central (Albert)	19/10/1916	21/10/1916
War Diary	E 11 Central	22/10/1916	30/10/1916
Heading	War Diary of Major J.J Griffith AVC A.D.V.S. 29th Division From 1st Nov 1916 To 30th Nov 1916 Volume 5		
War Diary	Corbie	01/11/1916	15/11/1916
War Diary	Treux	16/11/1916	18/11/1916
War Diary	A.2d. 9.7	19/11/1916	29/11/1916
Heading	War Diary of Major J.J.Griffith (A.D.V.S 29th Division From 1st Dec 1916 To 31st Dec 1916 Volume 6		
War Diary	A 2.d.9.7	02/12/1916	11/12/1916
War Diary	Corbie	12/12/1916	12/12/1916
War Diary	Oissy	13/12/1916	24/12/1916
Heading	War Diary of Major J.J. Griffith A.D.V.S. 29th Division From 4th Jan 1917 To 31st Jan 1917 Volume 7.		

War Diary		04/01/1917	06/01/1917
War Diary	Oissy	07/01/1917	11/01/1917
War Diary	Corbie	12/01/1917	16/01/1917
War Diary	A2d 9.7	17/01/1917	31/01/1917
Heading	War Diary of Major J.J Griffith A.D.V.S. 29th Division From 1st Feb 1917 To 28th Feb 1917 Volume 8		
War Diary	A2d 9.7	01/02/1917	09/02/1917
War Diary	Heilly	10/02/1917	21/02/1917
War Diary	Minden Post	22/02/1917	28/02/1917
Heading	War Diary of Major J.J. Griffith A.D.V.S. 29th Division From 1st March 1917 To 31st March 1917 Volumme 9.		
War Diary	Minden Post	01/03/1917	05/03/1917
War Diary	Heilly	06/03/1917	20/03/1917
War Diary	Oissy	21/03/1917	30/03/1917
Heading	War Diary of Major J.J. Griffith A.D.V.S. 29th Division From 1st April 1917 To 30th April 1917 Volume 10		
War Diary	Vignacourt	01/04/1917	01/04/1917
War Diary	Beauval	02/04/1917	02/04/1917
War Diary	Lucheux	03/04/1917	05/04/1917
War Diary	Bavincourt	06/04/1917	12/04/1917
War Diary	Agnez	13/04/1917	13/04/1917
War Diary	Arras	14/04/1917	26/04/1917
War Diary	Couin	28/04/1917	29/04/1917
Heading	War Diary of Major J.J Griffith A.V.C. A.D.V.S. 29th Division From 1st May 1917 To 31st May 1917 Volume 11		
War Diary	Arras	02/05/1917	31/05/1917
Heading	War Diary of Major A.B. Bawhay A.V.C. D.A.D.V.S 29th Division From 7th July 17 To 31st July 17 Vol 17		
War Diary	Field	07/07/1917	31/07/1917
Heading	War Diary of Major A.B. Bawhay D.A.D.V.S. 29th Division From 1st Aug 17 To 31st Aug 17 Volume 2		
War Diary		01/08/1917	15/08/1917
War Diary	Field	16/08/1917	31/08/1917
Heading	War Diary of Major A.B. Bawhay D.A.D.V.S. 29th Division From Sept 1st 17 To Sept 30. 17 Volume No 3		
War Diary		01/09/1917	30/09/1917
Heading	War Diary of Major A.B. Bawhay D.A.D.V.S 29th Division From Oct 1st 17 To Oct 31st 17 Volume No 4		
War Diary		01/10/1917	31/10/1917
Heading	War Diary of Major A.B. Bawhay A.V.C. D.A.D.V.S 29th Division From November 1st 17 To Dec 31st 17		
War Diary	Field	01/11/1917	28/02/1918
Heading	War Diary of Major A.B. Bawhay A.V.C. D.A.D.V.S 29th Division From March 1. 18 To March 31. 18 Volume 9		
War Diary		01/03/1918	31/03/1918
Heading	War Diary of Major A.B. Bawhay A.V.C. D.A.D.V.S 29th Division From April 1. 18 To April 30. 18 Vol X		
War Diary		01/04/1918	30/04/1918
Heading	War Diary of Major A.B. Bawhay A.V.C. D.A.D.V.S 29th Divn From May 1. 18 To May 31. 18 Vol XI		
War Diary		01/05/1918	31/05/1918
Heading	War Diary of Major A.B. Bawhay A.V.C. D.A.D.V.S 29th Divn From June 1. 18 To June 30. 18 Volume XII		
War Diary		01/06/1918	29/06/1918

Heading	War Diary of Major A.B. Bawhay A.V.C. D.A.D.V.S 29th Divn From July 1. 18 To July 31. 18 Volume X		
War Diary		01/07/1918	30/07/1918
Heading	War Diary of Major A.B. Bawhay A.V.C. D.A.D.V.S 29 Divn From Aug 13. 18 To Aug 31. 18 Vol XII		
War Diary		13/08/1918	31/08/1918
Heading	War Diary of Major A.B. Bawhay A.V.C. D.A.D.V.S 29th Division From Sept 1. 18 To Sept 30. 18 Volume 15		
War Diary	Wallon Cappel	01/09/1918	01/09/1918
War Diary	Hazebrouck	02/09/1918	07/09/1918
War Diary	Strazeele	08/09/1918	16/09/1918
War Diary	Vogeltze	17/09/1918	27/09/1918
War Diary	Brake Camp	28/09/1918	30/09/1918
Heading	War Diary of Major A.B. Bawhay A.V.C D.A.D.V.S 29 Division From Oct 1. 18 To Oct 31. 18 Volume No 16		
War Diary		01/10/1918	31/10/1918
Heading	War Diary of D.A.D.V.P 29th Division From 1/11/18 To 30/11/18 Vol 17		
War Diary		01/11/1918	30/11/1918
Heading	War Diary of Major A.B. Bawhay R.A.V.C. D.A.D.V.S 29th Division From 1/12/18 To 31/12/18		
War Diary		01/12/1918	31/12/1918
Heading	Rhine Army Southern Division Late 29th Division Dep. Asst Dir. Veterinary Services Jan-Oct 1919		
Heading	War Diary of Major A.B. Bawhay R.A.V.C. D.A.D.V.S 29th Division From Jan. 1.19 To Jan.31.19 Volume 19		
War Diary	Germany	01/01/1919	31/01/1919
Heading	War Diary of Major A.B. Bawhay R.A.V.C D.A.D.V.S 29 Division From Feb 1.1919 To Feb 28.1919 Volume No 20		
War Diary	Germany	01/02/1919	31/05/1919
Heading	War Diary of Major A.B. Bawhay D.A.D.V.S 29th Division For Month Ending 30 June 19 Volume No 24		
War Diary	Germany	01/06/1917	31/07/1917
Heading	War Diary of Major A.B. Bawhay R.A.V.C D.A.D.V.S Southern Division From 1/8/19 To 29/8/19 Volume No 26		
War Diary	Germany	01/08/1919	29/08/1919
War Diary	Berg Gladbach	01/09/1919	31/10/1919

Wolas / 22 90

13 Assiskent Director Volring Gesang

1916 mar — 1919 oct.

29TH DIVISION
DIVL TROOPS

A ST DIR. VETY SERVICES
MAR 1916 — OCT 1919

WAR DIARY
or
INTELLIGENCE SUMMARY

Army Form C. 2118.

ADVS 29th Division Vol 1/2

Place	Date	Hour	Summary of Events and Information	Remarks and references to Appendices
Camp	1916			

March 2nd 460th Battery left for Alexandria. Capt Armstrong A.V.C. in charge. Gave him instructions to draw his Vety equipment at Aley. Two other Batteries join this one before 132 Hotchkiss Rele.

March 3rd All artillery now complete as far as provide animal strength from R.E. Dn Train. Field Ambulances etc. Received Telegram re 10 A.V.C. Sgts. coming to join Batteries under new scheme. Saw Brig. Major R.A. about this.

March 4th Instructor M.V.S. to vaccinate Sgt & W2 20 V.H. 10 A.V.C. Sgts arrived from Abbassia Vety Hospital

March 5th Veterinary Stores arrived & distributed. Wallets yet to come.

March 6th 40 sick evacuated to 20 S.V.H. Wallets arrived & given out. Report 7 Rostings 7 A.V.C. Sgts sent to D.D.V.S.

March 8th 17th & 15th Brigades R.A. left. B Boylan A.V.C. upolne for duty re Capt Hyslop V.D. D in Train.

March 9th Inspected 147 Bde R.J.A.

March 10th 147 Bde R.J.A. left for embarkation. Posted War Diary for January. Went to Port Tewfik inspected 9th Corps animals.

Army Form C. 2118.

WAR DIARY
or
INTELLIGENCE SUMMARY.
(Erase heading not required.)

Summary of Events and Information 29th Division.

Place	Date	Hour	Summary of Events and Information	Remarks and references to Appendices
Suez Camp	1916 March 11th		Three A.V.C. Sgts arrived for 132 Bde R.A. from 21st S.V.H. Beileia attached them to Div H.Q. as 132 Bde has embarked. 18 M.V.S. embarked today from Port Tewfik on "S.S. Warilda."	
"	March 13th		Left Camp 7-30 a.m. for embarkation on S.S. Milliades from Port Tewfik. Capt Hyslop A.V.C. also embarked. Sailed 5 P.M.	
Port Said	March 14th		Remained here all day.	
At Sea	March 15th		2nd day at sea.	
"	March 16th		Kit Roll parade	
Marseilles	March 20th		Arrived this morning & disembarked 1 P.M. Left at 7 P.M. for Paris	
Paris	March 21st		Arrived here 9 a.m. Left again at 1-30 P.M. & arrived at Pont Remy at 5-30 P.M. & rang about 7 P.M.	
Long	March 22nd		Went to Pont Remy where M.V.S. was billeted. D.V.S. Cullen while out. Reported arrival to D.D.V.S. 4th Army.	
"	March 23rd		Gave circular letters Nos 45, 54, & 51 to all V.O.'S and read instructions re Remounts & horse affections. Impressed on all the necessity of + statistics re Remounts	

WAR DIARY
or
INTELLIGENCE SUMMARY.
(Erase heading not required.)

Army Form C. 2118.

Summary of Events and Information: 29th Division

Place	Date	Hour	Summary of Events and Information	Remarks and references to Appendices
Rong	1916		reduction of sick diseases. Inspected Div. hy. & animals	
"	March 23rd		Visited all Infantry Brigade Head Quarters	
"	March 24th		Very difficult to get Motor Car although one allowed for my use. Saw O.C. Div Train just joined Division. N.O.Yc St Venell.	
"	March 25th		D.D.V.S. Called & saw him & had long conference & made up procedure also the question of all animals to be "mallened" by the intra-palpebral method. Spoke to him re difficulty of Motor Car, but he does no road to interfere. Capts Stewart & Hyslop gone on leave this morning. Have Div Vestry published re inoculation of all sick & unfit to march. 12 Poole W.O. placed on the sick list.	
"	March 26th		Went to Port Remy & inspected all units there, also two at M.V.S. Went to Abbeville & called on D.V.S. remained for lunch & went on afterwards to W.O. 6 & 22 S.V. Hospital.	
"	March 27th		Sent two Cases Inspicions Mange from 86 to Abbeville.	
"	March 29th		Went to No 2 Advance Remt Depot & drew 13 chargers for H. Ameins, Brought Capt Armstrong, Lt Sewell & Pook to 22 S.V.H. Abbeville & had them inoculated in	

WAR DIARY or INTELLIGENCE SUMMARY

Army Form C. 2118.

29th Division

Place	Date	Hour	Summary of Events and Information	Remarks and references to Appendices
Long	1916		the intra-palpebral method of inoculation with "Mallein".	
Long	March 30th		went to Pont Remy & arranged move of M.V.S. to L'Étoile. Went to Villers-sous-Ailly & inspected animals Div. Train.	
	March 31st		Left Long for Beauquesne. M.V.S. move today, and removed to Abbeville.	
Beauquesne	April 1st		Capts. Stewart & Hyslop arrived on recall from leave. Pte. Hyslop in charge of 147 R.F.A. Bde. vice Rock. M.V.S. arrived then afternoon. Went to Acheux to see A.D.V.S. 36th Div. He was out.	
"	April 2nd		Sent Capt. Stewart to Beauval to take R.E. Coy. Went to Acheux & took over Office & M.V.S. hors from A.D.V.S. 36th Div.	
"	April 3rd		Arrived at Acheux from Beauquesne.	
Acheux	April 4th		Went to Domart where 9 inspected 15th 17th 147th Bdes R. Artillery	
"	April 5th		Inducted for Wallets for A.V.C. depts.	
"	April 6th		Inspected 19th Heavy Battery. This was the ground a number of cases of "Grease" & evidently not infection. Went to Mailly-Maillet where 9

Army Form C. 2118.

WAR DIARY
or
INTELLIGENCE SUMMARY.
(Erase heading not required.)

Summary of Events and Information 29th Division

Place	Date	Hour	Summary of Events and Information	Remarks and references to Appendices
Acheux	1916		Inspection W. Riding Coy. R.E. Very front standing by wall of chateau. Had a unit chest sent to this unit. 15th Bde R.A. move to Mailly today	
"	April 7th		Inspected 89th Field Ambulance & 86 Inf Bde Transport, at Rainsivall, also 16 Pioneers (R.I.R.) & 252 Tunnelling Coy. Salutes for 4 last Chots to replenish sanitary mes.	
"	April 8th		D.D.V.S. called and had long conversation on Officeral matters	
"	April 9th		Inspected 87th Field Ambulance at Mailly-Maillet. Complained to C.O. arrival from part on ground. Orders received that all arrivals in the Div Coln Mallinal V.D's informed of this	
"	April 10th		Mallinal Signals. Cold ration & animals on R.A. Head Quarters.	
"	April 11th		Went to Amplier inspected Div Train & 147 Bde R.A.	
"			Mallinal M.M. Police & Surrey Yeomanry detachment	
"	April 12th		Mallinal 89 Field Ambulance & R.E. Hd Qrs.	
"	April 13th		Inspected Police horses and A.P.M. 8th Corps Inspected Surrey Yeomanry. 132 Brigade R.A. & part of 17 & 15 Brigades at Amplier and Domart.	

Army Form C. 2118.

WAR DIARY
or
INTELLIGENCE SUMMARY.
(Erase heading not required.)

Summary of Events and Information 29th Division

Place: Acheux

Date	Hour	Summary of Events and Information	Remarks and references to Appendices
1916 April 14th to 16th		All V.O.'s now in possession of mallein & syringe & ready to begin inoculation of their units. 2 remounts arrived for the Div.	
April 16th		Took car out Belle Eglise 204 remounts for the Div.	
April 19th		D.D.V.S. called & raised the question of auto bus wheels for animals. 10% is allowed on animal strength of unit but arrange to get them.	
April 20th to —		Inspected sanitary arrangements horse lines. They are in a very bad state approximate the mallein & suspected glanders up soon.	
April 22nd		Inspected Transport of Newfoundland Regt. animals in good condition but lives very smartly.	
April 23rd		Sent all V.O.'s Army Vetped & vest instructions from D.V.S. re evacuation of useless animals — early collection of cases — horsing & nightly went out station Etc.? — All A.V.C. Sgt now in possession of Wallets.	
April 24th to 5th		371 Battery moved to Crum 46 area. Royal Scots & Munsters Machine Guns att. Divn. in	

Place	Date	Hour	Summary of Events and Information	Remarks and references to Appendices
Achiet	1916		April 25th to — Went on 5 days leave, first leave since leaving England on March 17th 1915. Capt Stewart C.V.C. performed duties of A.D.V.S. during my absence. During the many inspections made throughout the month I found it a common practice in a good many units to throw the grain ration on the ground. I had a Divisional order published on the 21st to the effect that it was wasteful, induces Debility, colic & that nose bags should be made full use of.	29th Division

T. J. Griffiths Major
A.D.V.S.
29th Div

WAR DIARY or INTELLIGENCE SUMMARY

Army Form C. 2118.

A.D.V.S. 29293

29th Division

Place	Date	Hour	Summary of Events and Information	Remarks and references to Appendices
Woking	1916			
	May 6th		Returned from leave. Inspected Park of Mange upstand to my Field Ambulance. Veterinary Microscopically showed Sarcoptic parasite. Cure reports.	
"	May 7th		Inspected 58 Inf. Bn. Transport. D.D.V.S. inspected Mobile Vety Section. Dept. Scott A.V.C. (Rtd) left mess for Base.	
"	May 8th		Visited Enfidaville, Mailly-Maillet, Remnant, Betancourt and Raincourt and inspected animals there. Visited 88 Field Ambulance at Archevé. Condition & lines of animals my front army & rear in Excellent	
			To my transport officer.	
"	May 9th		Inspected 13 Battery R.F.A. Condition of horses inspected also 16th Middlesex Regt Transport. My ford. Conference at Mons of D.D.V.S. Scheme discussed re Evacuation of Sick & wounded in next battle. Also question of Cracked & Grease Legs in heavy horses. Consulted Divisional Chief of the lines on legs. Called at Beauguesne on my way back to see Colonel Moore. Wrote O.C. Brigade & represented	
"	May 10th		Inspected 36 & 13 Battery only fair. Wrote letters received from him in the subject. - Inspected condition of animals	

Army Form C. 2118.

WAR DIARY
or
INTELLIGENCE SUMMARY.
(Erase heading not required.)

Instructions regarding War Diaries and Intelligence Summaries are contained in F.S. Regs., Part II. and the Staff Manual respectively. Title pages will be prepared in manuscript.

Place	Date	Hour	Summary of Events and Information	Remarks and references to Appendices
			29th Division	
Acheux	1916		29th Div Signals arrived, much help, & evidently more cases taken in hand.	
"	May 12th		Went to Amplier & inspected all Artillery units there. Change in General Composition taking place in D.A.C. + Div Train. the former to get units + the latter horses. Went to Belle Eglise & took over 158 remounts for Division. Survey Yeomanry left Division.	
"	May 14th		V.O. reports further case of Suspected mange in F.9 Field Ambulance. 4 Febr. returned from leave.	
"	May 15th		Capt Stewart OC M.V.S went on leave. I do his duty.	
"	May 17th		Inspected Div Train. Horses very good Condition. All under Canvas. Heavy. 10 Clyg. J. may for each Big horses not Enough. —	
"	May 18th		Sergt Smith W.C. (Clerk) return from furlough. No 1 Sect A.6 Reserve Park arrived Acheux arranged Vety attendance.	
"	May 20th		Inspected Section Reserve Park. Very good Condition. Inspection S.7 Machine Gun Section. Very dirty lines & animals. reported same to C.O. and arranged for another inspection.	
"	May 21st		Had a Conference with all V.O.'S re Evacuation of Sick and	

Army Form C. 2118.

WAR DIARY
or
INTELLIGENCE SUMMARY.
(Erase heading not required.)

 29th Division

Place	Date	Hour	Summary of Events and Information	Remarks and references to Appendices
Acheux	1916		Wounded animals in the event of hostilities on a large scale and read	
" "	"		to them scheme in course of preparation.	
" "	May 24th		Mobile Veterinary Section moved today to Rannevenent by order of G.O.C. I can see as no advantage for such move.	
" "	May 25th		Inspected 86th Machine Gun Section. Wy front Coulston, also 15th Battery. Capt Stewart returned from leave. Capt Thayill departed on leave.	
" "	May 26th		New A.S.C. clerk arrived. He knows very little of clerical work + writes indifferent. Sgt Scott will return to 18th M.V.S. by order.	
" "	May 27th		Inspection Wagon + Transport with C.O. Animals in good condition.	
" "	May 28th		Inspected Div Signal animals + T.M.P.	
" "	May 29th		Visited proposed collecting stations for wounded also early accessible tracks thereto. Inspected 358 & 460 Batteries.	
" "	May 30th		Inspected 87 Field Ambulance re reported mange. Scrapings showed Psoroptic. Two animals involved + have both sent to the Mobile Vety Station	

WAR DIARY or INTELLIGENCE SUMMARY

29th Division

Place	Date	Hour	Summary of Events and Information	Remarks and references to Appendices
Acheux	May 1916			
	May 30th		Saw Brigadier General R.A. and G.O.C. 87 Infantry Brigade regarding the collecting stations for wounded. Scheme to be submitted later. S/Sgt Scott. a.r.C. (clerk) transferred to 18 M.V.S. Saw staff Capt 87th Brigade re withdrawal of S/Sgt Knott a.r.C. During the month the condition generally of the animals has been well maintained. This is Ypres in part due to the amount of green fodder allowed. The quality of the hay & oats has been very poor.	
			J. J. Griffith Major A.D.V.S. 29th Div.	

Confidential

War Diary

of

Major J.J. Griffith A.V.C.
A.D.V.S. 29th Division

From 1st June 1916   To 30th June 1916

WAR DIARY or INTELLIGENCE SUMMARY

Army Form C. 2118.

(Erase heading not required.)

Instructions regarding War Diaries and Intelligence Summaries are contained in F. S. Regs., Part II. and the Staff Manual respectively. Title Pages will be prepared in manuscript.

Place	Date	Hour	Summary of Events and Information	Remarks and references to Appendices
ACHEUX	1916			
	June 1st		A good deal of shelling again today.	
"	June 2nd		Rode around by BEAUSART and MAILLY to see if there were better overland tracks where wounded could be got across.	
"	June 3rd		Inspected all transport animals at ACHEUX also 368 and 460th Batteries. The former yet not up to the mark, the other excellent. Inspected 89th Field Ambulance, not yet up to the required standard. Some horses dirty and shoeing not satisfactory.	
"	June 5th		Inspected Signal animals with C.O. Fair, good and hope this standard will be kept up. Put forward to A.A. & Q.M.G. my scheme for evacuation of sick in the event of hostilities.	
"	June 6th		Made a tour of different roads with O.C. M.T. and two N.C.Os. with a view to using same in case of many wounded arriving. Capt Magill R.V.C. returned from 8 days leave.	
"	June 7		Capt Armstrong off on 8 day leave.	
"	June 8th		Submitted scheme with map to A.A. & Q.M.G. re veterinary arrangements for evacuation of sick & wounded.	
"	June 10th		Scale war Diary for May. Went to Railhead to take over 3 mules and 17 chargers remount for Division	

Army Form C. 2118.

WAR DIARY
or
INTELLIGENCE SUMMARY
(Erase heading not required.)

Place	Date	Hour	Summary of Events and Information	Remarks and references to Appendices
ACHEUX	1916			
	June 11th		Inspected Heavy Artillery Group of animals at ACHEUX. Went to BUSY H Army with "evacuation scheme", had a long conversation re attendance on Heavy Artillery horses. I suggested a V.O. for a certain number of Groups and to under Corps	
"	June 12th		Posted divl sketch map to attack to evacuation scheme. Went to Conferences to see 88th Machine Gun Co. Inspected 87th Machine Gun Co. Not good, more experience required. NCOs in too young. Picked out case of mange	
"	June 14th		Visited all transport lines ACHEUX. Also some Heavy Artillery horses, found from Thousand Regt. Went to see some Heavy Artillery horses. On way picked up mail.	
"	June 16th		Inspected hore and found case of Skin disease in 11" 2 Section also a case in the trench Regt. Saw Cpl magt who appears not to take to clean their horses.	
"	June 17th		Had all V.Os to my offices and gave them copy of my scheme and then continued orders also their sources & desert covery. Had a telegram from HQ re conference tomorrow at his office. Showed all Vety officers Mange, tricks, and collecting stations where wounded will rally	

Army Form C. 2118.

WAR DIARY
or
INTELLIGENCE SUMMARY
(Erase heading not required.)

Place	Date	Hour	Summary of Events and Information	Remarks and references to Appendices
ACHEUX	1916			
	June 18th		Attended Conference at D.G.H. Office. It was decided to have ten men reinforcements from the Base to act as Orderly/runts and to be attached to 18 M.V. They are also available for 31st and 46th Divisions.	
	June 19th		Visited Section of 46th Reserve Park and K.O.S.B. transport at LOUVENCOURT. Saw Staff Capt. re transport Officer K.O.S.B. Shoeing very bad.	
	June 20th		48 Remounts arrived for the Division at Belle Eglise. N.O.R. Spoke to me about poor condition of animals D.A.C. in N°4 Section at AMPLIER. D.A.D.V.S. wired me to meet him at 36th Div tomorrow.	
	June 21st		D.A.D.V.S. spoke of poor condition of Dis Amm Col animals which he heard from A.D.R. Went to AMPLIER this afternoon to see those horses. Was horrified at their condition and picked out 38 for immediate evacuation for debility, more to follow. Very annoyed with Capt Hyslop, who is the Vety Officer, for keeping such animals. Notice board put up this day directing to collecting station. Saw O.C. 18 M.V.P. re reception of the above then horses and to arrange trucks. Sent to see Brigadier General R.A. about Dis Amn Col horses and their condition. N°4 Section being the only one with such thin and debilitated animals.	
	June 22nd		Interviewed O.C. Dis Amn Col re thin horses and stable management. Inspected Infantry Transport, Middlesex Regt, Essex.	

WAR DIARY or INTELLIGENCE SUMMARY

Army Form C. 2118.

Place	Date	Hour	Summary of Events and Information	Remarks and references to Appendices
ACHEUX	1916 June 22nd (Cont.)		88th Machine Gun Co, 146th Reserve Park and Heavy Artillery Battery. Went out to see supports all correct and in their right places. Inspected Newfoundland Regt and Lancs Fusiliers Transport.	
"	June 23rd		Inspected No. 1, 2, & 3 Sections 29th Divn Amm Col. All very good except No 3. Some of the horses not in good condition.	
"	June 25th		Govr called at my office and spoke about the condition of horses in No 4 Section Bus Amm Col. Sent a report explaining the reason. Inspected 88th Fd Amb, and found two crews of manges which I had immediately sent away. It appears that the Vety Officers have most cases of this kind on he cannot diagnose the disease of any kind and I have, on a previous occasion, spoke to A.D.V.S. about this Officers incapacitate. I visited MVS. He is getting too many kicks amongst he animals from the rear line of feet shackles.	
"	June 26th		Visited Collecting Posts all correct except for a want of chest defences at "A" post.	
"	June 27th		Visited 18th M.T. and sent two mules, admitted for debility back to their unit vers. No 1 Section Bus Amm Col	

WAR DIARY
INTELLIGENCE SUMMARY

Army Form C. 2118.

Place	Date	Hour	Summary of Events and Information	Remarks and references to Appendices
ACHEUX	June 27th (Cont) 1916		Private Johnson A.C. my Clerk, left for HAVRE this day. 96 Cheesecloughs and arrived in his place.	
"	June 30th		Visited M.V.S. one case of mange from N°2 Section Div. Am. Col. Visited the 3 Field Ambulance with M.O.M.'s very good except the 89th. Some of the heavy draught not in good condition and shoeing not up to the mark.	

During the month a large number of thin and unfit horses found their way into the Divl. Am. Col. by transfer from other units in the field and without Remount or Veterinary inspection. Units with thin and unfit horses would much prefer to load them on to other units in preference to sending them Sick. The increase in mange is mainly due to the inability of those concerned to early diagnose and segregate, and want of knowledge of the disease in general.

Moffett Major
A.D.V.S. 29th Dw

Vol 5

Confidential

War Diary

of

A. D. M. S. 29th Division

from 1st to 31st July 1916

Volume

Moffitt Major
a.D.M.S.
29th Div

A.D.V.S.,
29th Division.

Reference my No. A.753 dated 7/7/16. War Diary for July has not yet been received. This should be forwarded as early as possible so that the Diaries for the Division may be despatched to the Base without any further delay.

8th August, 1916.

W.C.Injom
Captain,
D.A.V. & Q.M.G., 29th Division.

O.T.D.

D.A.A. & Q.M.G.

Herewith War Diary for July
delay regretted

14-8
16

A.723
14.8.16

J.J. Esposito Major
A.W.V.S.

WAR DIARY
or
INTELLIGENCE SUMMARY

(Erase heading not required.)

Army Form C. 2118.

Place	Date	Hour	Summary of Events and Information	Remarks and references to Appendices
Acheux	1916 July 1st		Visited A & B Collecting posts. Everything correct.	
"	July 2nd		Arranged for night reliefs at collecting posts as it is possible casualties may occur at night.	
"	July 4th		The 2 Batteries and 1½ Sections S.A.C. of the 48th Division returned to their division.	
"	July 5th		Arranged for V.O. to visit 203rd Co. R.E. 36th Div. in MAILLY WOOD	
"	July 6th		Collecting posts withdrawn and signboards etc collected and brought in to M.V.S. S.A.C. moved to AMPLIER. D.D.V.S. Reserve Army called.	
"	July 8th		Went to AMPLIER and inspected S.A.C. Saw O.C. M.V.S. re move to ACHEUX. 69th Field Ambulance moving to ARQUEVES.	
"	July 9th		Went to 4th Army to see D.D.V.S. M.V.S. moved today from LOUVENCOURT to old lines at ACHEUX. Heavy Artillery Group moved to SARTON today	
"	July 10th		Inspected SWB and KOSB transport. Improvement in latters shewing. No transport Officer yet appointed	
"	July 11th		Inspected Worcester transport, took skin scrapings from itchy horse. Inspected No. 4 Section 46th Reserve Park. A very good lot. They arrived yesterday from ARQUEVES. Inspected Middlesex Transport, not so good as when I last saw them. Got correspondence re Court martial of Pte Holland AVC	

Army Form C. 2118.

WAR DIARY
or
INTELLIGENCE SUMMARY
(Erase heading not required.)

Instructions regarding War Diaries and Intelligence Summaries are contained in F. S. Regs., Part II. and the Staff Manual respectively. Title Pages will be prepared in manuscript.

Place	Date	Hour	Summary of Events and Information	Remarks and references to Appendices
ACHEUX	1916			
	July 13th		Went to ARQUEVES and inspected Farriers Wallets of Div. Train and 89th Field Ambulance, rather dirty, not properly kept, pointed same out to V.O. 54 remounts arrived for the Division, 35 for D.A.C. Not a good lot, condition might be better, pointed out same to A.S.R. Went to Brig. General R.A. re report of 3 horses transferred from 371 Battery to D.A.C. one alright and 2 in poor condition.	
"	July 14th		Arranged to inspect Farriers and A.V.C Sergeants wallets. Had to go to AMPLIER with Brig. Gen. R.A. re inspection of D.A.C. Capt Stewart inspected wallets and noted the deficiencies. On the whole they were good but some were dirty and drew attention of V.Os to this. Also deficiencies will in future have to be paid for unless a satisfactory explanation is forthcoming. Read out promulgation of Court Martial re Pte Holland and sent back correspondence to D.A.A.+Q.M.G. Fifteen thin horses of D.A.C. should be sent to M.V.S. for evacuation to L/E.	
"	July 15th		Attended Conference at D.A.V.S. Office RAINCHEVAL. Went to ARQUEVES and inspected 13, 26, and 92 Batteries R.F.A. Good condition and fairly well Shod. Inspected 460th Battery R.F.A. Very good	
"	July 17th		Had conversation with V.Os re importance early diagnosis of mange, wallets and their deficiencies, unit chests and the state of them and manner in which kept.	

WAR DIARY or INTELLIGENCE SUMMARY

Army Form C. 2118.

Place	Date	Hour	Summary of Events and Information	Remarks and references to Appendices
ACHEUX	1916			

July 18th A.D.V.S. visited and inspected M.V.S., 366th Battery and 88th Fd. Ambulance. Spoke about cases of mange recurring. Early diagnosis, isolation & disinfection most important. Gave him a copy of my late scheme for evacuation of wounded along with copy of Combined orders.

July 19th 3 Italy horses, H.Qrs. Stables. Ordered all animals outside stables and saw A.A. & M.G. on the subject. Stables thoroughly cleaned and disinfected and lime washed. I had 2 men from the Sanitary Section to spray the stables twice. Saddlery & rugs disinfected, bedding brushes & combs destroyed. Inspected Lancashire Hussars, Middlesex Transport, 97th and 15th Batteries. Went in evening to H.Qrs. Stables to see if cleaning and disinfecting was carried out. Parts left undone.

July 21st Went to ARQUEVE'S to see N.O. Co. 46th Reserve Park. Good condition. Went to H.Qr. stables re disinfection, better done this time. Inspected K.O.S.B. Transport. No 3 Section No. 6 left for AMPLIER

July 22nd Inspected all 88th Brigade Transport. Shoeing not too good.

July 23rd Orders re move from ACHEUX. Wired A.D.V.S. 25th Division re taking over and lines of M.V.S. 85 Remounts arrived for Division at 3.30am. I have already spoken to N.O.S.H. about horses arriving at the Lines. Went with Brig. General R.A. to see R.A. Remounts, all very good. One case of

WAR DIARY or INTELLIGENCE SUMMARY

Army Form C. 2118.

Place	Date	Hour	Summary of Events and Information	Remarks and references to Appendices
ACHEUX	1916		Marge. ADVS 25th Division came to see me.	
"	July 24th		One Sergeant and 9 men have arrived here from Base. Sent them on to ADVS 49th Division as per instructions from DDVS.	
"	July 25th		Received telegram re Influenza. Communicated same to all VOs. Left for BEAUVAL this morning.	
BEAUVAL	July 26th		Visited H.Qr animals, all correct. One horse 88th M.G.Co and one mule 86th M.G.Co left sick at BEAUVAL.	
"	July 27th		MVS arrived BEAUVAL this evening from ACHEUX.	
"	July 28th		Left BEAUVAL and arrived WORMHOUDT where I stayed the night.	
"	July 29th		Left WORMHOUDT and arrived HQrs about 10.30 am. MVS located with 6 Division MVS. Saw ADVS 6th Division not taking over and procedure in this Army. Went to HAZEBROUCK and reported arrival to DDVS. Had conversation re Mange. Slight cases can be treated.	
"	July 30th		Visited H.Qr horses, all correct except pony of D.A.QMG 3 Skin cases very much improved and still isolated.	

J Moffat Major
ADVS 29th Division

Confidential

War Diary

of

A.D.V.S. 29th Division

from 1st August 1916 to 31st August 1916.

Volume 2.

Moffitt Major
AVC

WAR DIARY or INTELLIGENCE SUMMARY

Army Form C. 2118.

Place	Date	Hour	Summary of Events and Information	Remarks and references to Appendices
POPERINGHE	1916			
	Aug. 1st		Inspected Border Regt. Transport, good. Ordered further Sulphur applications for Skin Cases in H.Qrs Animals	
"	Aug. 3rd		Inspected 86th Infantry Brigade Transport and Machine Gun Co. Shoeing bad and reported same to Q. Seven days leave approved owing to death of my father. Left for Boulogne Bridge this evening	
"	Aug. 12th		Left London on return from leave	
"	Aug. 13th		Arrived this morning for duty. Wrote Lieut SEWELL A.V.C. to attend to 3 Field Cos.	
"	Aug. 14th		Inspected 3 Field Cos. RE and 1/2 Pontoon Park RE Shoeing in Londons and Kent Co. not satisfactory. All animals in good condition. Skin Cases in HQr horses about better, ordered two to retake into work	
"	Aug. 15th		Inspected Divisional Train and Baggage animals attached to Infantry Brigade. All in good condition. 3 Cases of Suspicious Mange which I ordered to be sent to M.V.S. Recently joined remount mules not in good condition. Some recent issues of oats poor and dusty. Inspected No.4 Section D.A.C. Some mules with long feet Pointed this out to O.C. More shoeing smiths required	

WAR DIARY or INTELLIGENCE SUMMARY

Army Form C. 2118.

Place	Date	Hour	Summary of Events and Information	Remarks and references to Appendices
POPERINGHE	1916			
	August 16		Inspected 87th and 88th Infantry Bde Transport. Animals very good condition. Shoeing of some of the mules bad, too long feet, no preparation of foot before new shoe is put on. Sent a suspicious case of mange to M.V.S. Mules of this unit not in very good condition. Chargers ^from Worcester Regt. from 87th Bde HQrs sent Brigadier and Brigade Majors chargers to M.V.S. suspected mange. Saw civilian horse of DESIRE ZWANEPOEL a bad case of sarcoptic mange. Had his place put out of bounds and reported same to D.D.V.S.	
	Aug 17		Inspected Div. Signal. Good condition.	
	Aug 18		Inspected 88th Infantry Bde. Transport. Shoeing not yet satisfactory.	
	Aug 19		Inspected sick for evacuation at M.V.S.	
	Aug 20		Sent weekly report on condition of animals to A.D.V.S. Inspected 8th Field Ambulance, excellent condition of animals also shoeing. Visited WIPPENHOEK Siding. Capt Stewart V.O. Yo. Sick Horse train. Not enough trucks and some animals had to return to their lines. All mange cases sent.	
	Aug 21		Inspected 4 Batteries and 2 Sections 20th D.A.C. with V.O. in charge Capt Stewart returned from Sick Horse train duty.	

Army Form C. 2118.

WAR DIARY or INTELLIGENCE SUMMARY

(Erase heading not required.)

Place	Date	Hour	Summary of Events and Information	Remarks and references to Appendices
POPERINGHE	August 22nd 1916		Inspected Headquarters animals of 90th & 93rd Brigade R.F.A. also 7 Batteries R.F.A. 20 Divisional Artillery. Visited Hd. Qrs. Royal Irish and M.V.S. and ordered destruction of R.A. horse, pneumonia.	
"	August 23rd		Inspected Lancashire Fusiliers & K.O.S.B. Transport Showing improved but not yet up to the mark. Inspected the three Machine Gun Co. and 89th Field Ambulance. Shoeing not yet satisfactory. Animals in good condition. Nothing done in regard to the use of mange in Civilian Horse mentioned on 16th. Wrote D.D.V.S. pointing out the danger of such an animal and asking for further instructions.	
"	August 24th		at D.V.S. Inspected M.V.S. 87th and 88th Machine Gun Co. Monmouths. A 93 Battery, 1 Section D.A.C. and Divisional Train. Had a talk over Civilian Mangy Horse. A new pattern Gas helmet was tried but no decision come to. 99 Remounts arrived for the Division, a fair lot.	
"	August 25th		Visited M.V.S and 20th Div. R.A. H.Q. animals in excellent condition. One sick (wound Lacerates).	
"	August 26th		Visited Hd. Qrs. Horses. Inoculated Capt. Armstrong's charger with Anti Glanis Serum. Wound on Coronet.	

Army Form C. 2118.

WAR DIARY
or
INTELLIGENCE SUMMARY

(Erase heading not required.)

Place	Date	Hour	Summary of Events and Information	Remarks and references to Appendices
POPERINGHE	1916			
"	August 27th		Inspected Sick at M.V.S. for evacuation.	
"	August 28th		Report from O.C. B90 Battery RFA. Capt R D WILLIAMS A/C under arrest for drunkenness. Visited all units and inspected watering arrangements. Informed D.D.V.S. re Capt Williams A.V.C. and directed Lieut Alexander to do his duty.	
"	August 29th		Visited H Qr Horses, gave O.C. army report re watering arrangements in event of Glanders outbreak. Received private letter from B.G.R.A. concerning the case of Capt. Williams A.V.C. Consequence to mange in civilian horse received. Animal destroyed the day by owner.	
"	August 30th		Went to see B.G. R.A. re arrest and Capt Williams A/C. Capt Hyslop admitted Sick today, informed Division & asked D.D.V.S for relief. Capt. Stewart does his duty meantime.	
"	Aug 31st		Inspected Sick at M.V.S. arranged for the cleaning & disinfection of stable occupied by mangy horse belonging to DESIRE ZWAENEPOEL	
BRANDHOEK			Brought Capt Stewart with me to show him what is wanted done.	

Army Form C. 2118.

WAR DIARY
or
INTELLIGENCE SUMMARY

(Erase heading not required.)

Place	Date	Hour	Summary of Events and Information	Remarks and references to Appendices
POPERINGHE	1916		During the night 8th and 9th the enemy attacked with Phosgene Gas. 19 Animals were killed and others were rendered distressed, but recovered in a few days. One animal alone rapidly took flush and had to be evacuated. A new helmet is under trial which it is hoped will be effective against such poisonous gases.	

J Smyth Major
AVD. 29th D...

Confidential

War Diary

of.

Major J.J. Griffith A.v.C.   A.D.V.S. 29th Division

From 1st Sept. 1916   To. 30th Sept. 1916

Volume 3.

Army Form C. 2118.

WAR DIARY
or
INTELLIGENCE SUMMARY
(Erase heading not required.)

Instructions regarding War Diaries and Intelligence Summaries are contained in F. S. Regs., Part II. and the Staff Manual respectively. Title Pages will be prepared in manuscript.

Place	Date	Hour	Summary of Events and Information	Remarks and references to Appendices
POPERINGHE	1916			
	Sept 1st		Lieut. J. S. Keane A.V.C. (T.C) arrived in relief of Capt. Hyslop who evacuated to N°10 C.C.S.	
	Sept 2nd		Inspected 86th and 88th Infantry Brigade Transport animals. Gas alarm.	
	Sept 3rd		Inspected Sick at M.V.S for evacuation. Went to Sea cnes of suspected mange in 177th Tunnelling Co. R.E. not mange.	
	Sept 4th		Inspected the 3 Machine Gun Cos. All backward in shoeing and grooming, told Transport Officers to apply at once for shoeing Smiths and interviewed Staff Captain 86th Infantry Brigade on some Subject. Lieut G. Frayne A.V.C. arrived for duty with 20 Div. Artillery.	
	Sept 5th		Inspected 86th Field Ambulance. Very good. S/S J.2 Army called. Went to M.V.S inspected skin cases and advised special dressing. All doing well.	
	Sept 6th		Inspected 89th Field Ambulance. Shoeing bad, condition middling. Capt Cordy VIII Corps. V.O. called to his units.	
	Sept 7th		Inspected transport of Royals, Lancashire Fusiliers, Dublins, K.O.S.B. and 87th Field Ambulance. Heavy draught in Royals Cowing Condition, Shoeing Lancashire Fusiliers bad, Ambulance good.	

WAR DIARY or INTELLIGENCE SUMMARY

Army Form C. 2118.

Place	Date	Hour	Summary of Events and Information	Remarks and references to Appendices
POPERINGHE	1916		Sept 7th (Cont) Inspected Knuckling transport, very good. Visited 284 Co. R.E. He sick mule, evacuated same to M.V.S.	
"			Sept 8th 20th Divl Artillery start leaving today. Inspected 29th Divl Train very fair.	
"			Sept 9th Inspected M.V.S. and Hd Qr animals and sick for evacuation.	
"			Sept 11th Inspected the three R.E. Companies, Pontoon Park and Border Regt. transport, all very good. Shoeing of 1/12 London R.E. not so good, not so B.G.R.A. He tells me animals lost lot of condition. Visited 29th Divl Signals, not so good. They seem to be going back in condition. Informed C.O. Artillery arrived today, reorganising into 6 gun batteries, 132nd Brigade consequently broken up.	
"			Sept 12th Inspected Worcesters, Hants, Essex Newfoundland and HQrs 88th Brigade. All fairly good, and shoeing improved. Boyd's Army Called and had long conversation re mange dipping tanks and question of issue of dry rugs after dipping or blankets. Capt Fisher A.V.C. called and reported arrival. He informed me Capt Armstrong A.V.C. left behind sick. D.V.S. Circular Memo 45, 54, 84, 85, 86, 92, 97, 98, 99, 104, 105 and 107 sent to Lieut Keane for his information and	

WAR DIARY
or
INTELLIGENCE SUMMARY
(Erase heading not required.)

Army Form C. 2118.

Place	Date	Hour	Summary of Events and Information	Remarks and references to Appendices
POPERINGHE	1916		Sept 12th (Cont.) retention also report re Glanders and Nomenclature of Diseases	
"	Sept 13th		Capt Magill A.V.C. reported arrival. Inspected the three Machine Gun Co. 88th good except for shoeing, the other two bad and dirty mules. No shoeing Smith, 4th Gro Farrier helping with the shoeing by my orders.	
"	Sept 14th		Went to see about site for Mange dipping bath and suggested place near wooden bridge Switch Road. Saw AA & QMG on the subject. Inspected 4th Div Cook house re subject.	
"	Sept 15th		Inspected Nos. 4 & 2 Sections D.A.C. Horses not at all in good condition, about 100 cases of Debility, which must be evacuated. Saw O.C. on the subject. I think the animals must have been starved.	
"	Sept 16th		Inspected 15th Bde R.H.A. "Y" Battery the worst in all. About 50 cases of debility, the majority of which I was told came from the Batteries broken up.	
"	Sept 17th		Being 2 Army came to inspect D.A.C. on my advice. Nos. 2 & 4 Sections the worst, dirty horses and bad shoeing. He told me to get all the debilitated cases sent to L. of C. Stable management very bad.	

WAR DIARY
or
INTELLIGENCE SUMMARY

Army Form C. 2118.

Place	Date	Hour	Summary of Events and Information	Remarks and references to Appendices
POPERINGHE	1916		Sept 18th Went round O.V.C. with V.O. and picked out 119 animals allotted for evacuation and 12 from 15th Brigade R.H.A.	
"			Sept 19th Inspected 88th Infantry Brigade and 26th Battery, about 15 thin horses in the latter unit. Inspected Middlesex Transport and mule with Tetanus.	
"			Sept 20th 152 animals sick evacuated today. All practically littery.	
"			Sept 21st Visited 13th & 92nd Batteries, about 30 horses in the former and 35 in the latter all debilitated, very many dirty, stable management bad, no hay nets.	
"			Sept 22nd Visited HOUTKERQUE where I saw D/147 — 97th, and 10th Batteries. About 25 debility cases in the latter, 30 in 97th Battery and only 4 in D/147 Battery. Horses dirty, no hay nets and stable management appeared bad. Capt Armstrong AVC reports for duty today from the Base. Posted to 17th Bde R.F.A. and Capt Magill posted to 147th Bde.	
"			Sept 23rd Went to see D.D.V.S. at Hazebrouck and gave him report of debility cases in Batteries, also saw B.G. R.A on same report and it was decided to evacuate animals in two lots owing to such a large number.	

WAR DIARY
or
INTELLIGENCE SUMMARY

Army Form C. 2118.

Place	Date	Hour	Summary of Events and Information	Remarks and references to Appendices
POPERINGHE	1916			
	Sept 26th		17th Brigade R.F.a. Sect (9 horses) left today by train. Inspected 86th & 88th Brigade Transport, all fairly good. Shoeing of Lancashire Fusiliers not up to the mark. Visited 88th Field Ambulance & K.O.S.B. transport, both good.	
	Sept 27th		Inspected 87th Machine Gun Co. Mules dirty, no hay nets and about half the animals require shoeing. Visited Royal Inniskilling Fusiliers transport, animals fallen off in condition, shoeing backwork and no forage in the forage shed. No hay nets in either unit in use.	
	Sept 29th		Visited M.V.S. 26th Remount. arrive for Artillery and 12 H.D. for Divisional Train. Visited 89th Field Ambulance. Shoeing not up to date. Condition of animals good.	
	Sept 30th		Attended Conference at BAILLEUL by D.D.V.S. Principal subject control of Mange and location of dipping tanks. Calcium Sulphide appears to have many claims in the treatment of Mange but from my experience I fail to see it. Inspected Divisional Train. Animals very good indeed, clean, well groomed and fit for a good deal of work.	

Army Form C. 2118.

WAR DIARY
or
INTELLIGENCE SUMMARY

(Erase heading not required.)

Instructions regarding War Diaries and Intelligence Summaries are contained in F.S. Regs., Part II. and the Staff Manual respectively. Title Pages will be prepared in manuscript.

Place	Date	Hour	Summary of Events and Information	Remarks and references to Appendices
PoPERINGHE.			The condition of many of the Artillery horses on their repairing from the SOMME is very bad indeed. There seems to be a very bad system of stable management. Either forage was drawn short or it was wasted that the animals did not get it. The absence of hay nets was very noticeable and the consequent waste of hay was easy to observe. A positive pandemonium existed in N°4 Section D.A.C. on the visit of the D.D.V.S., horses were numerous over their food. Some were tied so short that they could not get at the hay, others entangled by the fore feet in ropes and chains and the stableman to release them. There was an absence of sufficient personnel to attend in the lines.	

Griffiths Major
a/9r.S. 29th to DW

2449 Wt. W14957/M90 750,000 1/16 J.B.C. & A. Forms/C.2118/12.

Vol 8

<u>Confidential</u>

<u>War Diary</u>

of

Major J.J. Griffith A.V.C.
       A.D.V.S. 29th Division

<u>From 1st October 1916</u>   <u>To 31st October 1916.</u>

<u>Volume H.</u>

WAR DIARY or INTELLIGENCE SUMMARY

Army Form C. 2118.

Place	Date	Hour	Summary of Events and Information	Remarks and references to Appendices
POPERINGHE (L'EBBE FARM)	1916 Oct. 1st		Wire received from D.D.V.S. re horse of 13th Battery RFA evacuated and reacted to Mallein test. Orders to test all animals of Battery.	
"	Oct. 2nd		All 13th Bty. animals inoculated with Mallein.	
"	Oct. 3rd		Inspected 13th Battery animals. All passed test and reported same.	
"	Oct. 4th		Orders received re move.	
"	Oct. 6th		Left L'EBBE FARM. Saw A.D.V.S. 55th Division and handed him over all papers, maps etc and routine of evacuation system in the 2nd Army. Called to see D.D.V.S. at HAZEBROUCK. He was out but left a note. Billeted in POPERINGHE this night.	
POPERINGHE	Oct. 7th		M.V.S. entrains this morning at 7am for SALEUX and march to CORBIE. Left PROVEN this day 7pm this day for SALEUX. Headquarters animals and Signal animals on train.	
CORBIE	Oct. 8th		Detrained and motor lorry to CORBIE.	
"	Oct. 9th		Orders received to move to RIBEMONT tomorrow.	
RIBEMONT	Oct. 11th		Arrived RIBEMONT. Went to see D.D.V.S at Army H.Q. quarters. 88th Inf. Brigade detached to 12th Division with 1/2 London Field Co R.E and N°H Section Div. Amm. Col. Our Artillery arrived this day in this area.	

WAR DIARY or INTELLIGENCE SUMMARY

Army Form C. 2118.

Place	Date	Hour	Summary of Events and Information	Remarks and references to Appendices
RIBEMONT	1916			
	Oct 12th		Went to see A.D.V.S. 12th Division re situation. Attended Conference at office of D.D.V.S. 4th Army. Principal Subject discussed was Veterinary arrangements and administration of Artillery of Division left in the line and evacuation of Sick. Arranged to leave one N.C.O and 5 men with the incoming Mobile Vety Section from the outgoing one.	
"	Oct. 13th		Capts. Fisher and Armstrong collect Vety stores arrived at M.V.S. and distributed to units concerned. G.O.C. did not approve of awards for Sergt Scott and Sergt Skinner. Correspondence returned to me on subject. 147th Brigade R.F.A move up to firing line. 86th and 87th Infantry Brigades to FRICOURT and MAMETZ.	
"	Oct 14th		Inspected three Companies of Divisional Train, very good. Went to see 12th Div Mobile Vety Section re taking over. Went to FRICOURT and saw 87th Brigade animals. No use made of Lay nets and many other Stable irregularities ie no attendance on lines etc, nosebags on empty, no picket ropes, oats on ground. Went to Artillery Camp ALBERT road. Saw 26th and 13th Batteries, fairly good. also saw part of Div Amm Col East Section now Ratied to form S.A.A. Sections with Infantry Brigades.	

WAR DIARY or INTELLIGENCE SUMMARY

Army Form C. 2118.

Place	Date	Hour	Summary of Events and Information	Remarks and references to Appendices
RIBEMONT	1916 Oct. 15th		Went to see DDVS re exchange of AVC Sergeants.	
"	Oct. 16th		Visited 86th Infantry Brigade. Same state of stable routine as 87th Brigade, no hay nets, no attendance on lines etc.	
"	Oct. 17th		Attended conference at DDVS office. Principal subject discussed was evacuation of animals. Different units are throwing additional units are thrown. A.Ds V.S. should notify each other of position of their M.V.S. In the case of Div" R.A remaining in the line when the Infantry of the Div" leave one N.C.O and 5 men should be detached to the incoming M.V.S. wrote AA & QMG re use of hay nets and got order published.	
E 11 Central (ALBERT)	Oct. 19th		left RIBEMONT for E 11 Central ALBERT.	
"	Oct. 20th		Sergt J.J. Scott A.V.C wounded in head (H.E) wired record for relief.	
"	Oct. 21st		Inspected the 3 Infantry Brigade Transport. Very good but the hard work is telling on them. Shoeing is very bad in 87 and 86th Machine Gun. Co. Reported Same to AA & QMG.	

Army Form C. 2118.

WAR DIARY or INTELLIGENCE SUMMARY
(Erase heading not required.)

Instructions regarding War Diaries and Intelligence Summaries are contained in F. S. Regs., Part II. and the Staff Manual respectively. Title Pages will be prepared in manuscript.

Place	Date	Hour	Summary of Events and Information	Remarks and references to Appendices
E. II Central	1916			
	Oct 22nd		D.D.V.S. called at office and referred to administration of Artillery left in the line. Sergt. Stevenson A.V.C. "L" Battery R.F.A. reported sick. Applied to records for relief. Capt MAGILL A.V.C. V.O. 147th Bde R.F.A. evacuated sick this day. Applied for two relief through D.D.V.S.	
	Oct 23rd		Visited 460 Battery R.F.A. Very good. Sent Sergt Bras A.V.C. from M.V.S. in temporary relief of Sergt Scott A.V.C. to 87th Inf Brigade. Went round all the Div Amm Col with V.O. All fairly good with exception of No 4 Section and from there I expect the most evacuations for debility.	
	Oct 24th		Went to see Lieut. 1st Australian Div" and thought him to See D.D.V.S. where arrangements were discussed re evacuation of Artillery sick left in the line when Division comes out.	
	Oct 25th		Went to POMMIERS REDOUBT again and saw 87th Infantry transport and 26th & 10th Batteries. Notice received re Lieut J L Sullivan A.V.C. who is to arrive in relief of Capt Magill A.V.C.	
	Oct 27th		Saw Lieut. 1st Australian Div re arrangements for returning and evacuations of sick belonging to 29, 41st & 12th Div Artillery. Sergt Fagg A.V.C. 26th Battery R.F.A. reported sick. Applied to A.V. Records for relief.	

WAR DIARY or INTELLIGENCE SUMMARY

Army Form C. 2118.

Place	Date	Hour	Summary of Events and Information	Remarks and references to Appendices
E.11.Corbal	1916			
	Oct. 29th		Orders received to move to BELLEVUE FARM. Cancelled later.	
"	Oct. 30th		Moved to CORBIE. Also Division this day and next.	

During the month I had to bring to the notice of Transport Officers the absolute necessity of using Haynets. The amount of hay that was being wasted was appalling and a Divisional Order now published giving effect to my views on the matter. The V.O. who arrived in relief of Capt. Magill appeared to have been ill before he left the Base. I am raising the question with the view that it would be a good practice to have V.Os. medically examined before coming from the Base in relief of Casualties at the front.

Whitfield Major
A.D.V.S. 39th Div.

Vol 9

Confidential

War Diary

of

Major J. J. Griffith Ave.
A.D.V.S. 29th Division

From 1st Nov. 1916 to 30th Nov. 1916

Volume 5.

WAR DIARY or INTELLIGENCE SUMMARY

Army Form C. 2118.

Place	Date	Hour	Summary of Events and Information	Remarks and references to Appendices
CORBIE	1916			
	Nov 1st		Lieut J.L. Sullivan arrived in relief of Capt J. Maguire and posted to 147th Brigade R.F.A.	
"	Nov 2nd		Inspected Royal Fusiliers Transport and 89th Field Ambulance. Inspected 29th Div. Signals, very good. Sent away 3 sick to M.D.S. for evacuation.	
"	Nov 3rd		120 remounts arrived for Division 2 H.D. for H Qrs, 20 H.D. for Div Train, 50 H.D. for artillery & 50 for Infantry Brigade. Inspected 1st Line Transport 86th Infantry Bde with C.O.s re Infantry Brigade. Inspected Vety Officers 147 Brigade sent Sect, sent correspondence re his illness and application for relief to D.D.V.S. Infantry Transport very good especially Middlesex Regt. Visited Kent R.E. very good. Saw Adjutant re water troughs and others on river banks.	
"	Nov 4th		Inspected 87th Brigade Infantry Transport, all very fair, also 86th Machine Gun Co. H.D. horses show most low in condition. Inspected S.A.A. Section 29th Div. Amm. Col. Mules very good. Some of the horses only fair. Had V.O. with me during inspection	
"	Nov 5th		Inspected 88th Bde Infantry Transport, all very good except Worcester Regt & they were bad. Have suggested to N.H. r Q.M.G. to take	

Army Form C. 2118.

WAR DIARY
or
INTELLIGENCE SUMMARY
(Erase heading not required.)

Place	Date	Hour	Summary of Events and Information	Remarks and references to Appendices
CORBIE	1916		Nov 5th (Cont) two L.D. from Newfoundland & Hants Regt and sent them to Worcester Regt being urgently in need to replace debilitated ones. Nov 6th Inspected 87th Machine Gun Co and 87th Field Ambulance, the latter very good but more supervision required in the Machine Gun Co. Animals not in good condition, only fair. Nov 7th Inspected Essex Regt and 88th Field Ambulance, all very good. Two sick removed from Essex transport to M.V.S. for evacuation. Nov 8th Inspected Divisional Train and 2 Cos. In very good stables and animals in very good condition. First issue of Veterinary Wallets and unit chests for Machine Gun Cos. Reduction of 2 tb hay into place from today. Saw A.A. & QMG and SSO on the matter. Animals must have full ration of hay. Nov 9th Inspected 87th Machine Gun Co. Very good camp on rise high ground, shoeing backward, more supervision required on lines, mules kicking each other. 73 Remounts for 6is RA handed over at Edgehill direct to R.A. Nov 10th Went to see DDVS 4th Army. Heard from ADR. that 73 horses were handed over at Edgehill station for Div Artillery 8/30 am previous	

Place	Date	Hour	Summary of Events and Information	Remarks and references to Appendices
CORBIE	1916		Nov. 10th (cont) morning. Spoke to D.D.V.S. about increased personnel for M.V. also reference new G.1098-89 Mobile vety Sections. G.S. limber wagons still down as 2.	
"	"		Nov. 12th. Visited front line Railhead. Met A.D.V.S. 8th Division. Saw his M.V.S. (15th), also 29th M.V.S. 17th Div. Both these units have lost their very bad situation. Ambulances through impassable roads and mud. Will send O.C. 18th M.V.S. to select another site probably near CARNOY.	
"	"		Nov. 13th. Inspected transport of Worcesters and Newfoundland Regts. Both good.	
"	"		Nov. 14th. Position of M.V.S. to be same as 8th Div M.V.S. Informed A.A.Q.M.G. the advisability of having horse ambulances and section horses in backward area E'10 Central, to which he agreed. As evacuations are daily becoming larger I have asked for 4 men of 29th Div Reserve Co to be attached to M.V.S. A.A.Q.M.G. agrees to this. I see no other place for 18 M.V.S. as all sites near main road have been taken by other units.	

Army Form C. 2118.

WAR DIARY
or
INTELLIGENCE SUMMARY
(Erase heading not required.)

Place	Date	Hour	Summary of Events and Information	Remarks and references to Appendices
CORBIE	1916			
	Nov 15th		Went to Conference at HQrs 4th Army. Discussed portions of M.V.S. under present conditions. It was agreed that M.V.S. should be at Railhead irrespective of units and collecting posts forward. Div. H.Q. moved today to TREUX	
TREUX	Nov 16th		Visited 17th Brigade R.F.A. D/17 Battery fairly good, 13th Bde. bad. 26th & 92nd Batteries fair. Many ration reduced to about 8 lbs. Cases of debility for evacuation are being kept owing to Strew of work this will ultimately entail larger wastage as a certain proportion of these may have to be destroyed and others evacuated so late as to render their fitness for further Service much longer delayed. Lieut J.S.Keane A.V.C. reported sick and evacuated to 21st C.C.S. Influenza. Relief applied for to D.D.V.S. Instructed Lieut Sewell to look after Infantry Brigade vice Lieut Keane A.V.C.	
"	Nov 17th		Capt J.M. Crowe A.V.C. arrived for duty and posted in temy charge 147/75th Bde R.F.A. vice Lt J.L. Sullivan A.V.C. Sick.	
"	Nov 18th		One mass of snow this morning. Went to Edgehill Station and issued 40 remounts for Division. Personnel of K.O.S.B. Inniskilling Fusiliers and Lancs Fus. did not turn up. Absence of these caused great inconvenience. Div. H.Q. moved to A.2.d.9.7.	

WAR DIARY or INTELLIGENCE SUMMARY

Army Form C. 2118.

Place	Date	Hour	Summary of Events and Information	Remarks and references to Appendices
A.2.d.9.7	1916			
	Nov 19th		Sergt. Scott A.V.C. reported for duty with 87th Inf Brigade this morning. Instructions issued to Sergt Brio hire to return to his unit (18 m.V.S.) Capt Gronse Ayre called at office and sent him to join his HQrs 147 Bde R.F.A.	
"	Nov 20		Visited 89th Field Ambulance and 87th Infantry Brigade transport. Spoke to G.O.C. re the effect of the mud on the Animals feet. Horse standings are to be cleaned of mud so that animals may stand on as dry ground as possible	
"	Nov 21st		Inspected 15th Bde H.Q. and 29th D.A.C. Large percentage of heavies held in No 1 Sec. Div. Am. Col. Requested the worst cases to be evacuated.	
"	Nov 22nd		Inspected 147 Bde R.F.A. 6 Bad feet in D/147 Bty and requested F.O.G. Lane have them evacuated early. Animals looking very well considering conditions.	
"	Nov 23rd		Visited 4th Div Arty, and 8th Div Arty & Div Amm Col. also m.V.S.	
"	Nov 25th		Visited 29th Div Arty, out of the line, camped at MEAULTE. 17 Div Arty Commn. in. Visited HQ R.A. Saw Staff Captain and told him debilitated animals were not being sent away.	

WAR DIARY or INTELLIGENCE SUMMARY

Army Form C. 2118.

Place	Date	Hour	Summary of Events and Information	Remarks and references to Appendices
A.2.d.9.7.	1916			
	Nov. 26th		4th Div. Arty. moved out of the line this morning. Went to Eaglehill and met remounts for Division (85) Train due at 9 am did not arrive until 5 pm and it was then dark. Leaving out remounts in the dark is much to be deplored and mistake must occur. Spoke to A.D.R. about this.	
"	Nov. 27th		Visited 88th Inf. Bde H.Q. Saw Brigade Major. Horse at no target. Septic wound, protest. Interviewed Sergt. Rymar re reference to a complaint from Brig. General Cayley. Visited 18 M.T. Then began Gun posts owing to dreadful condition of mud. Railhead Shalek which retarded evacuations. Submitted letter from O.C. 18 M.T. to D.D.V.S. reporting horses arriving at M.V.S. in advanced stages of debility. Artillery units being kept about Offendre, and specially reported to 4th Army letter No.1075 dated 11.11.16 para 4.	
"	Nov. 28th		Visited Kent R.E. advanced H.Qrs. & 86th M.G.Co. All animals very good except Machine Gun Co. mules which are falling off in condition. Accompanied patrol along MONTAUBAN – GINCHY – GUILLEMONT road. I really do not see the use of this patrol and will suggest its withdrawal. No two men would be much better employed at the M.V.S. to assist in the evacuation of sick to the Base.	

WAR DIARY
or
INTELLIGENCE SUMMARY

Army Form C. 2118.

Place	Date	Hour	Summary of Events and Information	Remarks and references to Appendices
A.D.V.S	1916		Nov. 29th Visited 87th Infantry Transport. All animals in fair condition except Machine Gun Co. mules show most falling off. Environment of Camp filthy and no attempt to make forage ways. Clearance of mud from standings commenced.	
			It is no wonder animal wastage is getting higher and higher, the awful conditions of mud and cold, the standings and no shelter will tell even heavier in the future, the conditions being apparent to all. Experiments with a piece of tin across the sole to prevent picked up nails is undergoing trial and up to the present it seems satisfactory. There has been a shortage of hay nets which does not help matters, as a good deal of hay has in consequence gone to waste.	
			Dec 2nd 1916.	

Whitworth Major
A.D.V.S. 29th Division

Confidential

War Diary

of

Major J.J. Griffith
A.D.V.S. 29th Division

From 1st Dec. 1916   To 31st Dec. 1916

Volume 6.

WAR DIARY or INTELLIGENCE SUMMARY

Army Form C. 2118.

(Erase heading not required.)

Instructions regarding War Diaries and Intelligence Summaries are contained in F. S. Regs., Part II. and the Staff Manual respectively. Title Pages will be prepared in manuscript.

Place	Date	Hour	Summary of Events and Information	Remarks and references to Appendices
A.2.d.9.7	1916		Dec 2nd. Visited 88th Infy Bde Hd Qrs. Saw Brigade Major and had conversation reference Sergt. R.H. Rymer Avre War Diary for Nov. Submitted to Q.	
			Dec 3rd Visited 88th Infy Bde H.Qrs. re unfavourable report on Sergt. Rymer.	
			Dec 4th. Went to Fourth Army HQ. to see D.D.V.S reference to Sergt. Rymer. Supply of Remounts and complaint from O.C. 18 M.V.S regarding treatment of men at No 7 Vety Hospital, one N.C.O. having been placed under arrest for going out in the town.	
			Dec 5th Visited 147 Brigade R.F.A. re report on road causing injuries to animals ie Sprains, shoes being pulled off. Saw C.R.E. who told me it would not be used much longer Decauville Railway would be available to bring the Ammunition up. Inspected 88th Infy Bde transport with Brigade Major, May nets not in use in any unit, hay being trampled under foot. Units had these nets but appear to keep them to look at only. Visited 18 M.V.S re Sergt Antony Avre 15t M.V.S.	

Army Form C. 2118.

WAR DIARY
or
INTELLIGENCE SUMMARY

(Erase heading not required.)

Place	Date	Hour	Summary of Events and Information	Remarks and references to Appendices
A.2.d.9.7.	1916 Dec. 6th		Interviewed Sergts. Gilmour and Rymer are visited 87th Inf Bde transport.	
"	Dec. 7		Visited 86th Inf. Bde transport and Divisional Train. Hay nets conspicuous by their absence. The only unit I saw them in use was the Div Train.	
"	Dec. 9th		Visited Div. Signal Co and H.Q. animals.	
"	Dec. 10th		Visited Div Amm Col., 15th Bde R.F.A. and Warwickshire R.H.A. Animals only in fair condition.	
"	Dec. 11th		Issued instructions to O.C. 18 M.V.S. to march to OISSY via CORBIE.	
CORBIE.	Dec. 12th		Div. H.Q. moved to CORBIE.	
OISSY.	Dec. 13th		Div. H.Q. moved to CAVILLON and OISSY. 18 M.V.S. arrived at OISSY. Not very good billets.	
"	Dec. 15th		Attended Conference at D.H.Q. Inspected H.Q.R.A. 2 animals to be evacuated.	
"	Dec. 17th		Visited MOLLIENS VIDAME. Saw 88th Fd Ambulance, Worcesters. Latter transport poor and dirty. On to MONTAGNE and inspected Essex transport	

Army Form C. 2118.

WAR DIARY
or
INTELLIGENCE SUMMARY
(Erase heading not required.)

Instructions regarding War Diaries and Intelligence Summaries are contained in F. S. Regs., Part II. and the Staff Manual respectively. Title Pages will be prepared in manuscript.

Place	Date	Hour	Summary of Events and Information	Remarks and references to Appendices
OISSY	1917			
"	Dec 17th (cont?)		Short of hay nets. Met animals drinking 12.50 p.m. first drink that day. Had conversation with Transport Officer on the subject. Essex transport animals only fair. More supervision required.	
"	Dec 19th		Inspected Royal Fusiliers. 1/3 Kent Field Co. R.E. 1/2 London Bn Co R.E. 87th Dy Bde transport and N° 3 Co. Divisional Train. All R.E. Co good, also Train.	
"	Dec 20th		Inspected Newfoundland, 88th Fd Ambulance, and 1/1 W Riding R.E. Two cutters, units good, Newfoundlands fair.	
"	Dec 21st		Inspected Lancs Fusiliers, Middlesex, R Dublin Fus, 86th Machine Gun Co. and N° 2 Co. Div? Train.	
"	Dec 22nd		Visited S.W. Borderers and 88th Field Ambulance. Fair. Animals only fed with hay once a day. I suggested this should be altered	
"	Dec 23rd		Inspected 88th Machine Gun Co. Very good.	
"	Dec 24th		Went on 10 days leave. O.C. 18 M.V.S. acting for me	

Army Form C. 2118.

WAR DIARY
or
INTELLIGENCE SUMMARY
(Erase heading not required.)

Instructions regarding War Diaries and Intelligence Summaries are contained in F. S. Regs., Part II. and the Staff Manual respectively. Title Pages will be prepared in manuscript.

Place	Date	Hour	Summary of Events and Information	Remarks and references to Appendices
			It seems impossible to make Transport Officers keep a certain percentage of hay nets and nosebags spare to replace worn out ones until they get supplied by Ordnance. A good deal of food is consequently wasted and never reaches the animals' stomach; another contributory cause of debility. J. Wright Major F.S. D.S. ADVS 29th Div	

2449 Wt. W14957/M90 750,000 1/16 J.B.C. & A. Forms/C.2118/12.

Confidential

War Diary

of

Major J. J. Griffith
A.D.V.S. 29th Division.

From 4th Jan.ry 1917   To 31st Jan.ry 1917.

Volume 7.

WAR DIARY or INTELLIGENCE SUMMARY

Army Form C. 2118.

Place	Date	Hour	Summary of Events and Information	Remarks and references to Appendices
	1917			
	Jan 4th		Arrived at Calais on return from leave where I had to stay until next day	
	Jan 5th		Left CALAIS 2/pm. arrived ABBEVILLE 10/pm. Left 12 midnight	
	Jan 6th		Arrived HANGEST 2.30am and got to OISSY 9 a.m. Conference at D.D.V.S. office this day. Did not attend. Sent Capt Stewart instead. Reported arrival from leave to 'Q' Branch and spoke about Veterinary lectures to Transport Officers.	
OISSY	Jan 7th		Inspected Divisional Train in Company with Commanding Officer	
"	Jan 8th		Capt Stewart's leave begins. Went to ABBEVILLE and saw D.V.S. Inspected 29th Div. Signals at PICQUIGNY owing to reported Mange.	
"	Jan 10		Wire received from Artillery, Capt Fisher Vice met with an accident from falling off his horse. Capt C. Armstrong AVC placed on the sick list. Wired Lieut-Keane Vice to proceed to MORLANCOURT and arrange evacuation of sick from 15th Bde R.H.A	
"	Jan 11th		Left OISSY for CORBIE. Called at D.D.V.S. on the way. Wired Lieut Keane to send Artillery sick to CORBIE for evacuation. Reported to 'Q' sickness of Capt Fisher and Capt Armstrong. A.H.Q at CORBIE.	

WAR DIARY or INTELLIGENCE SUMMARY

Army Form C. 2118.

Place	Date	Hour	Summary of Events and Information	Remarks and references to Appendices
CORBIE	1917. Jan 12th		Went to MORLANCOURT + saw 15th Brigade R.H.A. and Staff Capt. R.A. re illness of Vety. Officers. Reliefs applied for. 18 M.V.S. moved to CORBIE from OISSY. Went to EDGE HILL. 204 remounts arrived for Division. 151 of these for R.A.	
"	Jan 14th		Went to see Heavy Arty. at LA NEUVILLE. Inspected 125 Battery + arranged evacuation of their Sick. Gave Vety. wallet to their A.V.C. Sergt who had none. The wallet belonged to Sergt Epps A.V.C. Inspected 1/2 London Sth. Co. R.b. Good.	
"	Jan 15th		Inspected animals of Divisional School, very good, well kept, and well groomed. Sergt Aitken A.V.C. and my Clerk arrived from Eaure.	
"	Jan 16th		Left CORBIE, arrived A.a.d.9.7. 1pm. 18th M.V.S. arrived F.17d.9.9. Capt Crowe A.V.C. came to see me. Tried Casualty Clearing Station re Capt Fisher A.V.C.	
A.a.d 9.7	Jan 17th		Visited H.Qrs. 29th Divl Train. Went to MEAULTE but could not find No.1 Coy. Visited 18 M.V.S. Inspected 87th Fd. Amb. Good. Six inches of snow on ground.	
"	Jan 18th		Inspected No.1 Co. Divl Train. Seven sick evacuated. Went to H.Qrs Divn Amn Col. C.O. not there but saw the Adjutant. 3 Trucks of Sick evacuated by M.V.S. Thay. Lieut Sewell A.V.C. returned to duty from leave	

WAR DIARY or INTELLIGENCE SUMMARY

Army Form C. 2118.

Place	Date	Hour	Summary of Events and Information	Remarks and references to Appendices
A 2 d. 9.7.	1917			
	Jan 19th		Light fall of snow. 147 Bde R.F.A. and No 3 Sec. Div. Amm. Col. becomes Army Troops today. Wrote Staff Capt. R.A. for particulars. Saw G.O.C. with Sergt. Beckett A.V.C. re commission. Animals on ¾ ration from today.	
"	Jan 20th		Attended conference at D.O.V.S. office. Principal subjects discussed Stomatitis and administration of Corps Troops.	
"	Jan 21st		Visited 29th Div Signals, H.Q. R.E. and No 3 Co. Div. Train. Interviewed O/C Div. Train and Div. Amm. Col. Interviewed O/C about contagious Stomatitis also R.A. H.Qrs. on the same subject and re-organisation of Artillery. Two Batteries to cease & only one Section D.A.C. to become Army Troops.	
"	Jan 22nd		Visited Pack Cobs in forward area, 1/1 London Fd C.A.B., Newfoundland Regt, 87th Fd Amb., & 1/2 Monmouth Regt. In the case of the Pack animals no attention has been paid to the order re insertion of front cogs. In the other units mentioned front cogs will be inserted in the animals feet doing road work but not in those remaining in Camp.	
"	Jan 23rd		Visited 17th Brigade R.F.A., Worcesters, 87th Machine Gun C, Warwickshire R.H. Bty and "L" Batteries and Inniskilling Fus. Transport. Visited 29 Div Amm. Col.	

WAR DIARY or INTELLIGENCE SUMMARY

Army Form C. 2118.

Place	Date	Hour	Summary of Events and Information	Remarks and references to Appendices
A.2.Q.7.	1917			No 2 Section D.A.C.
"	Jan 23rd		(Cont') with C.O. Sergt. Millard A.V.C. reported for duty with No 2 Section.	
"	Jan 24th		Visited 147 Bde R.F.A. & No 3 Sec. D.A.C at MORLANCOURT, also 18 M.V.	
"	Jan 25th		Visited 29th Div. Signals. One horse dressed with skin dressing. Saw General Horse and inspected anti-tetanic Serum. Sent application to D.D.V.S. for School of Farriery at home.	
"	Jan 26th		Interviewed Vety. Officers at Office. Visited 88th Fd. Ambulance.	
"	Jan 27th		Saw General Horse	
"	Jan 28th		Visited Div. H.Q. Casualty report & Condition of Animals. Sent to Q. Visited M.V.S. and No 2 Co. Div. Train. Returned 2 cases of Supposed debility to R. Sub Div. Gave G.O.C. horse another injection of anti-tetanic Serum	
"	Jan 29th		15 Hay nets issued to Div H.Q. tried ones. Visited the 3 Field Co. R.E. and 1/2 Monmouth Regt. All very good. Sent Report to 15 G.R.A calling attention to waste of food. Stable errors, shortage of hay nets, rugs, nose-bags, and condition of animals. Gave as my opinion that a good many their animals were picketed in this way. Artillery camps too far from	

Place	Date	Hour	Summary of Events and Information	Remarks and references to Appendices
A.2.d.9.7.	1917		Jan 29th (Cont) the road and extra unnecessary work thrown on animals pulling G.S. and other waggons through 3 or 4 ft. of mud.	
"			Jan 30th Visited D/17 Battery. Animals fairly good. Also "B" Bty, animals only fair. No hay nets in use. No frost cogs in animals feet in either case.	
"			Jan 31st Conference at Army H.Qrs. Subject discussed Stomatitis and plans shewn and seen regarding exercise of horses. I raised the question of debilitated horses with a view to saddling responsibility on Unit Commanders. Sulphur and Oil dressing recommended for Canadian Ringworm on reports received regarding experiment on same	

WAR DIARY
or
INTELLIGENCE SUMMARY

Army Form C. 2118.

During the month the 147th Brigade RFA + No 3 Section Div. Ammn. Col. became Army Troops. The weather from the 16th has been very cold. Snow fell on night of 16-17 and has remained on the ground during the month. Freezing every night since the 17th and on some nights 20° of frost has been registered. The weather has been excellent for animals and wounds have healed much quicker than in milder weather. Evacuation of sick had to be held over for 5 days owing to shortage of trucks. Although frost ago were very essential owing to the slippery condition of the roads many units gave no attention to the G O C orders even when reported by me.

Sergt. Fa Beckett A.V.C., who was attached to 92nd Battery RFA, on recommendation and skeleton left the Division for England on the 29th to undergo training for temporary Commission in the Infantry.

MMrmth Maj R
ADMS 29 Div.

4-2/17

Vol 12

Confidential

War Diary

of

Major J. J. Griffith

A.D.V.S. 29th Division

From 1st Feb.y 1917   To. 28th Feb.y 1917

Volume 8.

Army Form C. 2118.

WAR DIARY
or
INTELLIGENCE SUMMARY.
(Erase heading not required.)

Instructions regarding War Diaries and Intelligence Summaries are contained in F.S. Regs., Part II. and the Staff Manual respectively. Title pages will be prepared in manuscript.

Place	Date	Hour	Summary of Events and Information	Remarks and references to Appendices
A2 d 9.7.	1916			
	Feb 1st		Visited 10th Reserve Park with A.D.V.S. Visited No 1 Section Div Amm Col. O.C. informs me that strength of animals 191 and average personnel to look after them is between 50 and 60. Capt Stewart informs me personnel very short in No 4 Section D.A.C. average 11 men to look after 74 animals at one period. The O.C. Section has Rev So.	
"	Feb 2nd		Interviewed V.Os at office. Visited HEILLY and went to 20th Division to ascertain about accommodation for M.V.S. when the Division moves here.	
"	Feb 3rd		Visited D.H.Q. and saw Generals. Issued D.R.O. 639 dated Feb 3rd stating only 3 ration of nets will be issued from Railhead from today.	
"	Feb 4th		Visited M.V.S. and 88th Field Ambulance. Latter unit perfect.	
"	Feb 5th		Visited TRONES WOOD and No 4 Section Div Amm Col. Good deal of hay wasted in lines and grain round forage Barns. They nets not being used in general. Unit says they are short. Holes in nosebags. Saw Section officer and pointed out these errors to him, also suggested animals going "up at night" should take Field Gp R.E., all very good. Visited the 117th Field Gp R.E. Removed 3 sick horses 5th (Gordon) Fd G. R.E.	

A5834 Wt. W4973/M687 750,000 8/16 D.D. & L. Ltd. Forms/C.2118/13.

WAR DIARY
or
INTELLIGENCE SUMMARY.
(Erase heading not required.)

Army Form C. 2118.

Place	Date	Hour	Summary of Events and Information	Remarks and references to Appendices
A29.7	1916			
	Feb 6		Capt Fisher reported for duty also Lt. J.J. O'Neill. The latter sent on to Morlancourt to take Capt Brown's place with 147 Bde RFA	
"	"		Capt Brown going to 17 Bde R.F.A. Inspected 13th Batteries, nosebags and rugs strewn carelessly about the lines in no section "A", "B" & and the general strewn with grain. Two horses had the nosebags tied round their necks and could not get at their grain. Spouted the out to the Battery S.M.	
	Feb 7		Inspected 17th Bde R.F.A. 92nd Battery S.M. states 27 men short. Scarcity of rugs and hay nets, animals fair. 13th Battery anemic fair. Scarcity of rugs. 26th Battery, animals only fair, show mis-want, all haynets down and animals feeding. Other appearance a batter Stable management in carried out. The other two Batteries haynets hung too low with the result that I saw some animals with the haynets entangled in their feet. Holes in nosebags thereby grain being lost	
"	Feb 8		Inspected Warwickshire R.H.A. Battery. Very good.	
"	Feb 9		D.H.Q. moved to HEILLY also 18th M.V.	
HEILLY	Feb 10		Distributed 32nd M.V.L (30th Division) Capt Scold Horses which should have been very dirty and no forage for remaining scat. No Nosebags left for sect.	

WAR DIARY or INTELLIGENCE SUMMARY

Army Form C. 2118.

Place	Date	Hour	Summary of Events and Information	Remarks and references to Appendices
HEILLY	1916			
"	Feb 11th		Visited 29th Div Signals and W Riding & Kent Field Coy R.E. Former unit is not very good. Something is going to going etc.	
"	Feb 12th		Visited HQ Div Train and Div MO	
"	Feb 13th		Visited 89th Infantry Bde Transport and N°1 and 3 Coy. His Train. All animals in fair good condition except Porters Regt Saw Brigade Commander at Frinvillers. Order regarding tin on horses feet not complied with 5 bad cases of debility to be evacuated, one ordered to be destroyed.	
"	Feb 14th		Inspected Horedates Transport very fair and enormously improved transport officers again charged. Inspected R Dublin Fusilers, Royal Fusiliers and Lancs Fus. All fair. Practice of putting a piece of tin across horses feet has become very strongly done in these units in fact it has become almost into disuse. Inspected 89th Field Amb Visited Merlincourt Coy 3 Bde RFA (20th Div) One Coy one Stomatitis ordered to be destroyed. Much work being done. Spoke to Lewis on the phone on the subject.	
"	Feb 15th		Inspected 149th (Kent) Field Coy R.E. & 455th (W Riding) Fld Coy R.E.	

Army Form C. 2118.

WAR DIARY
or
INTELLIGENCE SUMMARY.
(Erase heading not required.)

Place	Date	Hour	Summary of Events and Information	Remarks and references to Appendices
HEILLY	1916			
	Feb 16th		Visited CARDONNETTE, CoISY and RAINNEVILLE. Ants very good except some of the draught horses, on the poor side. Newfoundland Regt and 88th Machine Gun Co. good, horses on the poor side, a few very old amongst them. 88th Field Ambulance good. Truck Transport missing nearly all the mules clipped and looked very poor. Called at QUERRIEU and saw DDVS re Capt. Hermitoniece appointment and reports of Capt. Amos AVC to remain with	
"	Feb 17th		Visited D.H.Qrs	
"	Feb 19th		Visited MINDEN POST. Interviews with ADVS 17th Division re taking over and Conversation about Contagious Stomatitis. Saw to various list of units in attack chasses appeared	
"	Feb 21st		Div HQ moved to MINDEN POST	
MINDEN POST.	Feb 22nd		Inspected 18 M.V.S.	
"	Feb 23rd		Inspected Div Train. Good.	
"	Feb 24th		Visited Bronfay Farm 87th Inf Transport, No 5.B and Sw B. Good. Bronfillers and Border Regt only Train. Some of the stock looking very bad and left in practically a quagmire condition	

Army Form C. 2118.

WAR DIARY
or
INTELLIGENCE SUMMARY.
(Erase heading not required.)

Place	Date	Hour	Summary of Events and Information	Remarks and references to Appendices
MINDEN POST	1916 Feb 25th (Cont)		Saw Staff Captain 89th Inf Bngde regarding 5th Animals of Border Regt over strength. There are still 2 Mn animals in this transport. Visited BRIQUETERIE – BERNAFAY Rd and myself 86th and 88th Inf Bde. transport. Saw mules still in the same condition as last reported. Royal Fusiliers – no work being done on the stables, men lounging about. Transport Officer and Transport Sergt not to be found. I find with the exception of the Middlesex and Kents Regts my suggestion that ropey rugs on clipped animals has not been carried out. Visited 1/5 Monmouth Regt and the three Field Coys R.E. Animals on the whole good. There is a very bad approach to these units, very muddy and dangerous. There is no proper arrangements for watering these and. Watering out of shell holes already polluted with human excreta &c. Went to Camblas to see C.R.E. but found that his Camp was at ARROWHEAD COPSE.	
	Feb 26th		Visited 15th Bde R.H.A. and Div Amm Col. Warwickshire ? 460th Batteries fair. "B" & "F" Batteries only fair. 29th D.A.C. No 2 Section good, No 4 Section missing. Nos 1 and 3 Section fair. Suggested to each O.C. unit the necessity of keeping the rugs on clipped out animals. Complaints were made about dirty oats. Samples being produced which contained foreign particles such as pieces of iron, grit, and dirt	

Army Form C. 2118.

WAR DIARY
or
INTELLIGENCE SUMMARY.
(Erase heading not required.)

Instructions regarding War Diaries and Intelligence Summaries are contained in F.S. Regs., Part II. and the Staff Manual respectively. Title pages will be prepared in manuscript.

Place	Date	Hour	Summary of Events and Information	Remarks and references to Appendices
MINDEN POST	1916			
	Feb 27th		Visited 17th Brigde R.F.A. 92nd and 13th Batteries. 26th Bty good. Stabling. There seems to be bad stable management in this unit. Old Corn sacks used for nosebags and hung by wire on to animals on examining some nosebags over 20% were unserviceable from holes at the bottom and sides. It appears the animals go out on duty in the early morning get no water until their return back to the lines. O.C. inform me that there is no opportunity to water. Suggests that nosebags should be carried also on animals that go out on the early morning duty.	
	Feb 28th		Conference at Office of D.D.V.S. South Army. Subject discussed relation of Keters, in M.V.S and necessity of A.D's V S two Charges.	

A5834 Wt.W4973/M687 750,000 8/16 D.D.&L. Ltd. Forms/C2118/13.

WAR DIARY
or
INTELLIGENCE SUMMARY.

Army Form C. 2118.

Place	Date	Hour	Summary of Events and Information	Remarks and references to Appendices
	2.2.17		From my observations it appears a good deal of food is wasted through faulty nosebags and very little attempt made to keep them in repair. This was quite noticeable in Artillery units and this with the evident shortage of personnel to properly look after animals is no doubt a very possible cause in the production of debilitated animals. There is again the question of water. In unit Ammunition Cord animals that leave the lines early in the morning get no water until they return in the afternoon. Above remarks communicated to B.G.R.A in a separate report.	J.H.Hyett Major ASVC, 29th Div

Vol/3

Confidential

War Diary

of

Major J. J. Griffith
A.D.V.S. 29th Division

From 1st March 1917   To 31st March 1917

Volume 9.

WAR DIARY or INTELLIGENCE SUMMARY

Army Form C. 2118.

Place	Date	Hour	Summary of Events and Information	Remarks and references to Appendices
MINDEN POST	1917			
	March 1st		Visited Div. HQ. CRE and part of Signal Animals. Reported to CRE large wastage of hay and filthy stables.	
"	March 2nd		Visited Nov. 20th Division re handing over site of 18 M.V.S. Arranged with 'Q' that M.V.S. moves on the 4th to HEILLY. Submitted War Diary for Feb. to 'Q'. Visited R.A. HQ Lorries.	
"	March 5th		Div. HQ. moved to HEILLY	
HEILLY	March 6th		Visited CRE animals. Inspected HQ transport and 29th Div Signal.	
"	March 7th		Visited N. Riding & Kent Field Co. R.E. Both good.	
"	March 8th		Inspected 88th Infantry Brigade Transport in company with Brigade Major and Acting Brigadier. Worcester transport still only fair but general cleanliness and routine seems to be improved. Newfoundland animals very good, Essex mules thinner since last report. My suggestion to the Transport Officer that he should keep his cliffed mules rugged whether in open or under cover was not acted upon. Three mules have recently been lost from debility and there are about ten more which I consider at present unserviceable from the same cause. I consider the Transport Officer to blame for this state of affairs as he took no steps to protect this mules from the inclemency of the weather. The lorries of this transport are only fair. Monmouth and 88 Field Ambulance good.	

WAR DIARY
or
INTELLIGENCE SUMMARY

Army Form C. 2118.

Place	Date	Hour	Summary of Events and Information	Remarks and references to Appendices
HEILLY	1917			
	March 9th		Inspected 86th Brigade Transport. VILLE. Royal Fusiliers good, Royal Dublin Fus. good but I noticed 4 or 5 mules with head-galls. Middlesex, very good. Lancs Fusiliers, good. Some mules require shoeing. 86th Machine Gun Co. good but 2 clipped mules standing without their rugs on.	
"	March 10th		Inspected 87th Brigade Transport. Very good except Inniskilling Fusiliers. K.O.S.B. a few breast galls for which I suggested Steepter and saw OC on the subject. Called at Brigade HQ and saw Brigadier and gave him my remarks about his transport. Still complaints about animals being off their feed. 87th Field Ambulance, very good. 3 horses short of establishment.	
"	March 12th		Went to Edgehill and viewed 156 Remounts for Division and 60 for Div. R.A.	
"	March 13th		Visited 29 Div. Signals, made suggestion of dressing to be used on harness (mixture of Whale Oil & Soft Soap) Visited H.Q. R.6	
"	March 14th		Inspected 88th Brigade Transport. Newfoundlands + Hants good. Worcesters have improved since last report and now good. Even debilitated mules have now been evacuated. The remaining clipped mules were still without rugs when I visited the lines today. Report on this transport to be sent to "Q".	

Army Form C. 2118.

WAR DIARY
or
INTELLIGENCE SUMMARY.
(Erase heading not required.)

Instructions regarding War Diaries and Intelligence Summaries are contained in F. S. Regs., Part II. and the Staff Manual respectively. Title pages will be prepared in manuscript.

Place	Date	Hour	Summary of Events and Information	Remarks and references to Appendices
HEILLY	1917			
	March 15th		Visited 86th Brigade Transport.	
"	March 17th		Visited 89th Brigade Transport.	
"	March 19th		Conference at D.D.V.S. Fourth Army Office. Subjects discussed, Evacuation, Horse rugs etc.	
"	March 20th		Div. H.Q. moved to CAVILLON and OISSY.	
OISSY	March 21st		18 M.V.S. arrived at OISSY. Inspected Signals 'Q' 'phoned O.C. to meet Essex Regt. tomorrow. Inspected No. 4 Co. Div. Train.	
"	March 22nd		Inspected 88th Brigade Transport. Destroyed 2 horses of Essex, one aged + debilitated and bad case of ulceration. Cellulitis and proposed taking 6 more away. Interviewed Staff Captain and 'Q' regarding this Transport	
"	March 23rd		Visited R. Dublin Fus. + Div. H.Q.	
"	March 24th		Visited ALLERY, LEQUESNOY, RIENCOURT, TAILLY and ARRAINES. Inspected what was left in of S.W.B. Hants and Royal Fusiliers, these units were on parade full day and most of their transport was out. 89th F.A. Ambulance good but 3 horses getting debilitated. 86th M.G. Co. Several animals showing in to stables without their rugs on. Animals fair Inniskilling Fusiliers.	

A 8834 Wt. W4973/M687 750,000 8/16 D.D.&L. Ltd. Forms/C.2118/13.

WAR DIARY
or
INTELLIGENCE SUMMARY

Army Form C. 2118.

Place	Date	Hour	Summary of Events and Information	Remarks and references to Appendices
OISSY	1917			
	March 25th		Visited 88th Field Ambulance, Worcester Regt. and 88th M.G.Co. All good especially the Ambulance animals.	
"	March 26th		Visited the three Field Coo. R.E. Div HQ and M.M.P. animals. All good but 455th (M.Kilkeny) Fd. C. the best.	
"	March 28th		Infected Lanes Fus., Middlesex, travelling two. Dublin Fus. temporarily few.	
"	March 30th		DHQ moved to VIGNACOURT also 18th M.V.S.	

The following points I brought to notice of "Q". Hay & straw purchased locally for animals, no information is sent to D.O. units as to the amount available for issue.

Informed as to the question of early evacuation of debility animals brought up at D.O.V.S. conference on the 19th.

Informed Q that ¾ ration is not enough for heavy draught horses.

M.M.Mills Major
A.D.V.S. 29th Division

Confidential

War Diary

of

Major J.J. Griffith

A.D.V.S. 29th Division

From 1st April 1917   To. 30th April 1917

Volume 10.

Vol 14

Army Form C. 2118.

WAR DIARY
or
INTELLIGENCE SUMMARY.
(Erase heading not required.)

Instructions regarding War Diaries and Intelligence Summaries are contained in F. S. Regs., Part II. and the Staff Manual respectively. Title pages will be prepared in manuscript.

Place	Date	Hour	Summary of Events and Information	Remarks and references to Appendices
VIGNACOURT	1917			
	April 1st		D.HQ. moved to BEAUVAL. XVIII Corps wire full ration of Grain for Artillery animals.	
BEAUVAL	April 2nd		D.H.Q. moved to LUCHEUX	
LUCHEUX	April 3rd		Submitted March War Diary to 'Q'.	
"	April 5th		D.H.Q. moved to BAVINCOURT	
BAVINCOURT	April 6th		Inspected S.A.A. Section D.A.C. Animals fair. Ignorance displayed as to amount of forage to be drawn. Correct amounts do not appear to be known by unit Commanders. Too much latitude given to subordinates in this matter.	
"	April 7th		Visited 15th Bde R.H.A. 17th Bde R.F.A. 29th & 26th Amm Col. GROVE S. Animals only fair. Told V.Os to evacuate all unfit animals for debility. This would be roughly about 140. Absence of Hay nets and consequent great waste of hay. Saw the B.G. R.A. during my inspection and told him this. Almost all unclipped animals standing without rugs on them. Some units said they had none and indents on D.A.D.O.S. had not been complied with. Other said animals eat them and it is impossible to keep the supply up, but on enquiries I found no provision was made to prevent animals from eating rugs.	

WAR DIARY or INTELLIGENCE SUMMARY

Army Form C. 2118.

Place	Date	Hour	Summary of Events and Information	Remarks and references to Appendices
BAVINCOURT	1917			
	April 8th		Inspected D.H.Q. and 87th Field Ambulance.	
"	April 9th		Inspected 86th Infantry Bde transport. 497th (Kent) Fd Coy R.E. 86th M.G. Co. and Border Regt.	
"	April 10th		Inspected 88th Infantry Bde transport except horses while on line of march. All fairly good. Inspected 89th Fd Ambulance good, also No.4 Section Fd Amn Col. Animals only fair. 3 worn out M.D. in ambulance waiting to be replaced by remounts.	
"	April 12th		D.H.Q. moved to AGNEZ also 18 M.V.T.	
AGNEZ	Apl 13th		R.H.Q. moved to ARRAS. Animals on full rations from today	
ARRAS	Apl 14th		Inspected 15th Bde R.H.A. & 17th Bde R.F.A. 138 animals for medical examination in these two Brigades. Reported the 6 B.G.R.A. these still appear to be a good deal of wastage of horses in R.A. units. Shortage of hay Nets. General stable management appears to be bad. 15th Brigade animals evacuated without any comment but correspondence received re 17th Bde. Animals and obstacle put in the way.	
"	April 15th		Inspected 87th Infantry Brigade & 455th (N. Riding) Fd C. R.E.	

Army Form C. 2118.

WAR DIARY
or
INTELLIGENCE SUMMARY.
(Erase heading not required.)

Place	Date	Hour	Summary of Events and Information	Remarks and references to Appendices
ARRAS	1917			
	April 16th		Inspected 29th Div Sig Coy. S, 88th Inf Brigade Transport 510th (London) Fd C.A.b. No 2 Co. 29th Div Train.	
"	April 17th		Inspected 86th Inf Brigade	
"	April 18th		Inspected 497th (New) Fd C.R.b. + 455th (W Riding) Fd C.A.b.	
"	April 19th		Visited 86th Inf Bde. good. Arranged for 18th M.V.S. to send mounted patrol daily between ARRAS and TILLOY to collect derelict animals and hand over to Advanced A.V.C. Post at ARRAS.	
"	April 20th		Visited FREVENT and moved 161 Remounts for Divisions. Visited 18th M/S	
"	April 21st		To ST POL to see D.D.V.S. who was not in.	
"	April 22nd		Inspected 29th Div Train. Good.	
"	April 23rd		Inspected 86th Infantry Brigade + three Field C. R.b.	
"	April 24th		Inspected 15th Bde R.H.A., 17th Bde R.F.A. + 29th Div Amm Col. 127 animals noted for evacuation for debility and other causes pending arrival of Remounts and tactical situation, and 61 from Infantry Brigades and other units.	
"	April 26th		Div HQ moved to COUIN.	
COUIN	April 28th		M.V.S. arrived at COUIN. 127 Remounts arrived for Division.	

Army Form C. 2118.

WAR DIARY
or
INTELLIGENCE SUMMARY.
(Erase heading not required.)

Place	Date	Hour	Summary of Events and Information	Remarks and references to Appendices
COUIN	1917 April 29th		Inspected 29th Div. Sig. Coy. E. & S.A.A Section 29th Div. Very heavy casualties from shell fire during the month, total 278. The full forage ration has made a difference in the general condition but cases of debility in far too large numbers still occurs in Artillery units. Stable management must be bad and food wasted which should have been consumed, same reported to "Q". The Veterinary Patrol on the Arras-Tilloy road did very good work in collecting animals which would otherwise have been lost. They were nearly all Cavalry animals and it appears little or no provision was made for their collection by Cavalry M.V.S's. when the Cavalry left the line.	

M. Mitchell Major
A.D.V.S
29th Div.

Confidential

War Diary

of

Major J. J. Griffith A.V.C.
A.D.V.S. 29th Division

From 1st May 1917 to 31st May 1917.

Volume II

WAR DIARY
or
INTELLIGENCE SUMMARY.

(Erase heading not required.)

Army Form C. 2118.

Place	Date	Hour	Summary of Events and Information	Remarks and references to Appendices
ARRAS	1917.			
	May 2nd		D.H.Q. moved to Arras.	
	May 4th		Submitted War Diary for March. Applied to D.D.V.S. for reply for Pte Aitken reverted to permanence. Rode Kent R.E.	
	May 5th		Inspected 29th Dn.F. and 3 Infantry Bde. Remounts to Riding R.E. & London R.E.	
	May 6th		No 30093 Pte Sergt Aitken H.A.V.C. reverted to Pte & returned to No 2 Vety Hospital.	
	May 7th		Visited 17th R.F.A. & 15th Bde R.F.A. animals for Debility which were Refused but to accepted one with D.D.V.S. instructions dated 2/10/17. Some have been evacuated.	
	May 8th		D.H.Q. moved to Warlus from Arras.	
	May 9th		Visited 18th M.V.S.	
	May 10th		Visited 29th Divisional Train Animals Group.	

WAR DIARY or INTELLIGENCE SUMMARY

Army Form C. 2118.

Place	Date	Hour	Summary of Events and Information	Remarks and references to Appendices
ARRAS	1917			
	May 12th		Visited 86th + 87th Infantry Bdes.	
	May 15th		D.H.Q. moved to ARRAS + Sr. V. S. Establishment saw D.D.V.S. 3rd Division re. Loading over from him.	
	May 16th		Inspected M.M.P. and Divisional Train.	
	May 17th		Visited M.V.S. with O.C. M.V.S. in pointing out patients but 86 invalids when they could go to the water trough, they after first started to feed and looked after for first.	
	May 18th		Inspected 86th, 87th + 88th Infantry Bde. Inspected 86th over Sudden Lameness and turned good except Sudden Lameness. This was reported in my weekly animal report to Q.	
	May 19th		Inspected Sgt. Ma C. Do Remounts for Div Arty + 72 for Div Eng were duly arrived.	

WAR DIARY or INTELLIGENCE SUMMARY.

(Erase heading not required.)

Army Form C. 2118.

Place	Date	Hour	Summary of Events and Information	Remarks and references to Appendices
ARRAS	10/17			
	May 20th		Inspected 15th Bde R.H.A. + 17th Bde R.F.A.	
	May 21st		Visited D.D.V.S. Third Army.	
	May 22nd		Visited M.V.S.	
	May 25th		Visited 1/3 Monmouths.	
	May 26th		Visited 3 Field Coy R.E. and Infantry Rest Camps.	
	May 27th		23 Remounts arriving for Divisional Artillery. Visited Remount issues for Artillery.	
	May 28th		87 Remounts arrived for Artillery + Div. C Visited 87th, 88th + 89th Field Ambulances	
	May 29th		Divn. Sanitary Sec. A.V.C. reported no departure on leave.	
	May 30th		Visited M.V.S. & gave notes to M.V.S.	
	May 31st		D.D.V.S. 3rd Division gave M.V.S. taking over from Captain	

WAR DIARY
or
INTELLIGENCE SUMMARY.

Place	Date	Hour	Summary of Events and Information	Remarks and references to Appendices
ARRAS	1917		1st to V.S. inspected Police Horses, very good.	
			During the month 1500 Anti Gas Helmets were issued for the ammunition of the Divisional Ammunition Column, these were unable given to all concerned by the Divisional Gas Officer, along with the Very best instruction. The animals of the Division have continued to keep their condition in a satisfactory state. No forage and cattle rations had to be supplied to Forage and cattle rations distributed by the grazing. Sick again animals have not been numerous but which on the whole is very much on the decrease lately. Evacuations of animals continue to be principally due to the facts of having systematically nearly all their divisor ammunition animals.	

J.M.Griffith Major
A.D.V.S. 29th Div.

Confidential

War Diary
of

Major A. B. Bowhay A.V.C.
D.A.D.V.S. 29th Division.

From 7th July 17   To 31st July 17.

Army Form C. 2118.

WAR DIARY
or
INTELLIGENCE SUMMARY.
(Erase heading not required.)

DADVS.
29th Division

Instructions regarding War Diaries and Intelligence Summaries are contained in F.S. Regs., Part II. and the Staff Manual respectively. Title pages will be prepared in manuscript.

Place	Date	Hour	Summary of Events and Information	Remarks and references to Appendices
Field	7.7.17	9.30pm	Arrived at 29th Div. H.Q Abt. [?] Appointment of DADVS reported my arrival DHAQMG	#B13
	8.7.17		Reported my arrival in person to ADVS X Corps. Went through orders received filed in this Office	#B13
	9.7.17		Inspected 2016 M.V.S. Had a meeting of all V.O's in 29th Division	#B13
	10.7.17		Inspected all animals of 88th Inf. Bde. and of 29th Divisional Train	#B13
	11.7.17		Accompanied ADVS X Corps on his inspection of 29 DAC. Made arrangement to have all sight mange cases in contact in the Division dipped in Army skin dip	#B13
	12.7.17		Inspected 15th Bde animals	#B13
	13.7.17		Made up weekly Veterinary Report	#B13
	14.7.17		Attended conference of DADVS' at ADVS (XIV Corps) Office. Inspected animals of no2 Coy DAC. Rendered Vet. report for week ending for Div Commander	#B13
	15.7.17		Inspected animals of HdQts. Div Police, Div Signals	#B13
	16.7.17		Inspected animals of Hrs trsp Coys R.E, - 86th Inf. Bde - and mange cases of 1/2 Monmouthshire Regt.	#B13
	17.7.17		Inspected animals of 17th Bde R.F.A	#B13

H.B.Bowhay
Maj DADVS 29th Division

Army Form C. 2118.

WAR DIARY
OR
INTELLIGENCE SUMMARY.

(Erase heading not required.)

D.A.D.V.S.
29 2 Division

Instructions regarding War Diaries and Intelligence Summaries are contained in F. S. Regs., Part II. and the Staff Manual respectively. Title pages will be prepared in manuscript.

Place	Date	Hour	Summary of Events and Information	Remarks and references to Appendices
Field	18/4/17		Inspected mange cases in D.M.C. in No 4 Coy Div Train. Accompanied A.D.V.S. on his inspection of mange cases in 1/1 Monmouthshire Regt & 26 Batt R.F.A. Also some cases of poisoning (gas) which were admitted to No 16 M.V.S. this morning. The V.O. in charge was treating two of the worse cases.	ABO ABO
	19/4/17		Visited lines, which had been vacated by units well skin disease among their animals. Many of these had been disinfected satisfactorily	ABB
	20/4/17		Had a meeting of V.O.s of the Division & discussed very arrangements for coming active operations. Inspected animals of 87 2 Inf Bde.	ABB
	21/4/17		Attended conference of A.D.V.S. at the office of A.D.V.S. XIV Corps. moved with Div H.Q. to a new area. Rendered weekly dysy report return for Div Commander.	ABB
	22/4/17		Inspected animals of S.A.M. Section D.M.C.	ABB
	23/4/17		Inspected animals of No 229 H.Q. Coy which had just come out from England	ABB
	24/4/17		Inspected all animals stationed in the Division which have been formerly through a course of dipping for skin disease – with the exception of artillery animals	ABB
	25/4/17		Accompanied A.D.V.S. on his inspection of mange cases in the Div. Artillery animals	ABB

F.R. Bowlay Capt
D.A.D.V.S. 29 Division

Army Form C. 2118.

WAR DIARY
or
INTELLIGENCE SUMMARY.
(Erase heading not required.)

D.A.D.V.S.
29th Division

Instructions regarding War Diaries and Intelligence Summaries are contained in F. S. Regs., Part II. and the Staff Manual respectively. Title pages will be prepared in manuscript.

Place	Date	Hour	Summary of Events and Information	Remarks and references to Appendices
Field	26/4/17		Inspected animals of 87 & 89 Field Ambulances. And those of aeroplane Reps especially for chaney which was bad on my last inspection.	ADB
	27/4/17		Had a meeting of V.O's of the Division. Inspected animals of L Batty 26" Battery	ADS
	28/4/17		Attended conference of DADVS' at the office of ADVS XIV Corps. Handed weekly Vety return report for the Commander.	ADB
	29/4/17		Nothing to note.	ADB
	30/4/17		Inspected animals of 88th Inf Bde.	ADB
	31/4/17		Inspected animals of No 1 Coy Div Train. Visited wagon lines of Div Artillery in forward area. Saw late arrangements were correct.	ADB

A.B.Bowhay
Major AVC
DADVS 29 Division

War Diary
of

Major A. B. Bowhay
D.A.D.V.S. 29th Division

From 1st Aug 17.   To 31st Aug 17.

Volume 2.

Army Form C. 2118.

WAR DIARY
or
INTELLIGENCE SUMMARY.
(Erase heading not required.)

DADVS
29th Division

Instructions regarding War Diaries and Intelligence Summaries are contained in F. S. Regs., Part II. and the Staff Manual respectively. Title pages will be prepared in manuscript.

Place	Date	Hour	Summary of Events and Information	Remarks and references to Appendices
	1/8/17		Visited sick lines of several units.	AAB
	2/8/17		Visited sick lines of units not visited yesterday.	AAB
	3/8/17		Had a meeting of VOs. re the guinea suo de out weekly returns	AAB
	4/8/17		Attended Conference at ADVS Office - Rendered weekly report to Divisional Commander.	AAB
	5/8/17		Inspected animals of 1/1/2 Hampshire Regt.	AAB
	6/8/17		Inspected animals of 1st Kent RE Coy.	AAB
	7/8/17		Inspected animals of 86 & 2 Inf Bde	AAB
	8/8/17		Moved to another area with Div. Hd Qrs. Inspected animals of RHQ	AAB
	9/8/17		Inspected animals of 17 Bde RFA	AAB
	10/8/17		Had a meeting of VOs of the Division - made out weekly returns	AAB
			Inspected animals of Div. train.	
	11/8/17		Attended Conference at ADVS office - Rendered weekly report to Divn Commander. Inspected animals of 1st & 2nd & 3rd Field Ambulances in back area	AAB
	12/8/17		Inspected animals of Div. H.Q. Cb.	AAB
	13/8/17		Inspected animals by Div. Signal Coy. + those of Kent RE, London RE, West Riding RE Coys	AAB
	14/8/17		Accompanied ADVS in visits on his inspection of 15 & 2nd Bde RHA.	AAB
	15/8/17		Inspected animals of 87th Inf Bde	AAB

A.B. Bowley
Major RAVC
DADVS 29 Divn.

Army Form C. 2118.

WAR DIARY
or
INTELLIGENCE SUMMARY.   D.A.D.V.S.
(Erase heading not required.)   29th Division

Instructions regarding War Diaries and Intelligence Summaries are contained in F.S. Regs., Part II. and the Staff Manual respectively. Title pages will be prepared in manuscript.

Place	Date	Hour	Summary of Events and Information	Remarks and references to Appendices
Field	16/8/17		Visited Sick lines of several units.	A.B.B.
	17/8/17		Visited Sick lines of other units not visited yesterday. Held a meeting of V.O's - made out weekly returns	A.B.B.
	18/8/17		Attended conference at AD V S office - made out weekly report for Div. commander.	A.B.B.
	19/8/17		Saw all vety Sergeants & explained what I wanted them to do in their units. Examined horse vety wallets	A.B.B.
	20/8/17		Visited R.F.A lines with a view of picking out horses which wanted a rest	A.B.B
	21/8/17		Inspected animals of 88nd Fd Ambulance.	A.B.B
	22/8/17		Inspected animals of D.A.C	A.B.B.
	23/8/17		Inspected animals of 17th Bde R.F.A.	A.B.B.
	24/8/17		Had a meeting of V.O's of the Division - Made out weekly returns. Inspected animals of 1/1/2 Monmouth Regt.	A.B.B.
	25/8/17		Attended conference at AD V S office. Re-examined MDVS to find evacs for Divisional M.T. & Corps cavalry station.	A.B.B.
	26/8/17		Inspected animals of Div Signal Troop	A.B.B.
	27/8/17		Inspected animals of 117th Bde R.F.A with C.O. 17th Bde.	A.B.B.
	28/8/17		Inspected animals of Vent & Corps R.E	A.B.B.
	29/8/17		Moved to another area with Div Hd Qts.	A.B.B.

A.B. Barclay
Major D.A.D.V.S 29th Div.

Army Form C. 2118.

WAR DIARY
or
INTELLIGENCE SUMMARY.

(Erase heading not required.)

Instructions regarding War Diaries and Intelligence Summaries are contained in F. S. Regs., Part II. and the Staff Manual respectively. Title pages will be prepared in manuscript.

Place	Date	Hour	Summary of Events and Information	Remarks and references to Appendices
Field	30/6/17		Inspected Animals of 6th 2 Inf Bde.	A123
	31/6/17		Inspected animals of 329 H.Q. Coy.	A123

J.B. Bowsher
Major
D.A.D.V.S. 39 Division

Vol 19

War Diary
of
Major. A. B. Bowhay.
D.A.D.V.S. 29th Division

From Sept. 1st. 17   To Sept. 30. 17.

Volume No 3.

WAR DIARY
or
INTELLIGENCE SUMMARY.
(Erase heading not required.)

Army Form C. 2118.

DADVS 29th Division

Place	Date	Hour	Summary of Events and Information	Remarks and references to Appendices
	1/9/17		Inspected animals of 86th Infantry Bde.	A.B.B
	2/9/17		" " " of Div Signal Coy	A.B.B
	3/9/17		" " " of R.E. Coys	A.B.B
	4/9/17		Went on leave to England	A.B.B
	5/9/17		Reported Divsn from leave	A.B.B
	10/9/17		Visited Sick lines in amb. seeing all DOs	A.B.B
	11/9/17		Inspected animals of Div train	A.B.B
	17/9/17		Inspected animals of 87th Inf. Bde.	A.B.B
	18/9/17		Inspected " " of 15th Bde R.H.A	A.B.B
	19/9/17		" " 17th Bde R.F.A	A.B.B
	20/9/17		Inspected animals of DAC made out weekly returns	A.B.B
	21/9/17		Attended conference at ADVS office - moved areas with Div H.A.	A.B.B
	22/9/17		Visited sick lines of some units	A.R.C
	23/9/17		Took over charge of DMVS while officer i/c on leave for 10 days	A.B.B
	24/9/17		Inspected animals of 86th Bde.	A.B.B
	25/9/17		Inspected 3 Companies RE.	A.B.B
	26		Inspected Animals of 1/1 Monmouthshire Rgt.	A.B.B

A.R.Brothers Maj
DADVS 29th Division

Army Form C. 2118.

WAR DIARY
or
INTELLIGENCE SUMMARY.
(Erase heading not required.)

Instructions regarding War Diaries and Intelligence Summaries are contained in F. S. Regs., Part II. and the Staff Manual respectively. Title pages will be prepared in manuscript.

DADVS 2nd Division

Place	Date	Hour	Summary of Events and Information	Remarks and references to Appendices
	27/9/17		Visited sick lines of some units	AB.B
	28/9/17		Had a meeting of VOs in the Division and the ord weekly returns.	A.B.B.
	29/9/17		Attended conference at ADVS Office. Inspected animals of 227 neg. By.	AB.B
	30/9/17		Visited sick lines of some units	AB.B

H B Bowskay
Maj
DADVS 2nd Division

War Diary
of
Major A. B. Bowhay D.A.D.V.S
29th Division

From Oct 1st 17   To Oct 31st 17

Volume No 14

Army Form C. 2118.

WAR DIARY
or
INTELLIGENCE SUMMARY.

(Erase heading not required.)

S.A.D. v.S. 29th Division

Instructions regarding War Diaries and Intelligence Summaries are contained in F.S. Regs., Part II. and the Staff Manual respectively. Title pages will be prepared in manuscript.

Place	Date	Hour	Summary of Events and Information	Remarks and references to Appendices
	1/4/17		Inspected animals of 86th Inf. Bde.	A.S.S.
	2 Aug 17		Inspected	A.S.S.
	3		" " " Bde. R.H.A.	A.S.S.
	4		" " 17th Bde R.F.A.	A.S.S.
	5		Visited transport lines of several units. Same site for erection of Lines.	A.S.S.
	6		Inspected animals of Glasgow Light Infantry who had just joined the Division	A.S.S.
	7		Attended Conference at office of A.D.V.S. XIV Corps	A.S.S.
	8		Visited sick lines of 1st Field Ambt.	A.S.S.
	9		Inspected animals of 89th & 90th Ambulances	A.S.S.
	10		" " of 3 ?? Coys R.E.	A.S.S.
	11		Had transport horses inspected throughout the Division	A.S.S.
	12		Visited sick lines of some units	A.S.S.
	13		Held a meeting of V.Os in the Division. made out weekly effort returns	A.S.S.
	14		Attended conference at office of ADVS XIV Corps. Inspected animals 87 Inf Bde.	A.S.S.
	15		Inspected animals of Bob Squab, Police. Hqrs etc.	A.S.S.
	16		Inspected animals of 86 & 87 Inf Bde.	A.S.S.
	17		moved from XIV Corps area to VI Corps area with Division	A.S.S.

W.R.Bison R.A.V.C. Major
DADVS 29th Divn.

Army Form C. 2118.

WAR DIARY
or
INTELLIGENCE SUMMARY.
(Erase heading not required.)

DADVS 29th Division

Instructions regarding War Diaries and Intelligence Summaries are contained in F. S. Regs., Part II. and the Staff Manual respectively. Title pages will be prepared in manuscript.

Place	Date	Hour	Summary of Events and Information	Remarks and references to Appendices
	16/1/17		S.I. and I. to ADVS. Reported arrival to ADVS VI Corps	A.B.1.
	18/1		Inspected animals & Provisional trans	A.B.1.
	19/1		Made out weekly report returns - visited Transport lines of some units	A.B.1.
	20/1		Attended conference at office of ADVS VI Corps	A.B.1.
	21/1		Visited sick lines of cable units	A.B.1.
	22/1		Accompanied ADVS VI Corps on his inspection of 16 M.T.S.	A.B.1.
	23/1		Accompanied ADVS VI Corps on his inspection of 9th & 19th & 58th "Duf" Bdes	A.B.1.
	24/1		Inspected animals of 3 Corps R.E., 327 M.G. Coy.	A.B.1.
	25/1		Inspected 58th "Duf" Bde.	A.B.1.
	26/1		Held a meeting of V.Os. of the Division - made out weekly report return.	A.B.1.
	27/1		Attended conference at office of ADVS VI Corps. Inspected animals of 22nd 4th M.A.S.	A.B.1.
	28/1		Visited q.d. Co. of 2nd Cavalry, attached, and purchased the Service	A.B.1.
	29/1		Inspected animals of D.T.H.Q.	A.R.1.
	30/1		1/5 Bde R.H.A.	A.B.1.
	31/1		17 R.F.A.	A.B.1.

ABBostock Maj Veterinary
DADVS 29 Division

War Diary
of

Major. A. B. Bowhay. A.V.C.
D.A.D.V.S. 29th Division

From November 1st 17
To ~~Dec 31st 17~~ ~~February 28 18~~

Army Form C. 2118.

WAR DIARY
or
INTELLIGENCE SUMMARY.

(Erase heading not required.)

DADVS. Vol 5 29th Division

Place	Date	Hour	Summary of Events and Information	Remarks and references to Appendices
Field	1/4/17		Visited sick lines of sous units	ARB
	2/4/17		Held a weekly of VOs of the Division. Made out weekly reports & returns	ARB
	3		Attended conference at office of ADVS VI Corps.	ARB
	4		Inspected No 3 & 4 Coys Div Train, Div M.G. Coy.	ARB
	6		Attended inspection of HQrs VI Corps of some units in the Division.	ARB
	7		Inspected animals of 87 & 88 Inf Bde.	ARB
	8		Inspected " of R. Guernsey Lt Inf, Pnr Facilities	ARB
	9		Held a meeting of VOs of Division. Made out weekly report & returns.	ARB
	10		Inspected animals of D.A.C.	ARB
	11		Attended conference at Office of ADVS 6th Corps. Inspected animals of Div HQrs Div Signal Coy RE, Police, Motor Boats.	ARB
	12		Inspected animals of 15th Bde R.H.A.	ARB
	13		" 17th Bde R.F.A	ARB
	14		" 88 2nd Inf Bde.	ARB
	15		" 1/2 Monmouthshire Pioneer Batt & Div MG Coy.	ARB
	16		Went to Railhead & distributed remounts received to units of Division.	ARB

A B Bosh 4th Mch
DADVS 29th Div.

WAR DIARY or INTELLIGENCE SUMMARY.

Army Form C. 2118

DADVS 29th Division

(Erase heading not required.)

Instructions regarding War Diaries and Intelligence Summaries are contained in F.S. Regs., Part II. and the Staff Manual respectively. Title pages will be prepared in manuscript.

Place	Date	Hour	Summary of Events and Information	Remarks and references to Appendices
	17/11/17		Moved from VI Corps area to III Corps Area	A 13.13
	18		Attended conference at ADVS' office III Corps. Inspected 3 Fd Coys R.E.	A 13.13
	19		Moved to new area with Div HQ Sh. Had a meeting of VOs of Division	A 13.13
	20		Inspected water supply for horses in Div Camps.	A 13.13
	21		Selected site for a Div Vety Post. Inspected water supply in forward area. Rendered report.	A 13.13
	22		Visited a Div Vety Post. Inspected all pack animals in forward area.	A B.E.
	23		Held a meeting of VOs of Division. Made out weekly return & report.	A 13.13
	24		Inspected animals of Div H.Q. Sh. Div Signal Coy R.E. & Police	A 13.13
	25		Inspected all Inf. Transport animals.	A 13.13
	26		Inspected animals of DAC	A 13.13
	27		" " " 2 Bde RHA	A 13.13
	28		" " " 15 Bde RHA	A 13.13
	29		Visited Div Vety Post. Inspected animals of 1/1 Lowland Mtd Bgde & Pioneers Bn. Inspected animals of Div R.F.A.	A 13.13
	30		Gave Orders for 18 N.C.O.s & men to a camp party to the area for the a Div Vety Post to take its place	A B.D.

ADP Barclay Major
DADVS 29 Division

Army Form C. 2118.

WAR DIARY
or
INTELLIGENCE SUMMARY.
(Erase heading not required.)

Vol 6

DADVS 29th Division

Place	Date	Hour	Summary of Events and Information	Remarks and references to Appendices
	1/12/17		Made out weekly reports returns	AB.B
	2		Ordinary routine work. Inspected animals of Div HQ Coy.	A.B.B
	3			A.B.B
	4			A.B.B
	5		Moved to III Corps area to IV Corps Area.	A.B.B
	6		Visited office of ADVS IV Corps. reported arrival. Met & saw Div. transport	A.B.B
	7		Held a meeting of V.O's of Div. Made out weekly reports returns. travel part.	ACB
	8		Inspected 3 Fd Coys R.E.	A.B.B
	9		Inspected animals of 86th Inf Bde.	A.B.B
			Inspected animals of Div H.Q ab. Signal Coy R.E. & Police	A.B.B
	10		" " of 15th Bde R.H.A.	A.B.B
	11		17 Bde R.F.A.	
	12		D.A.C	A.B.B
	13		88th Bde & 1/2 Monmouthshire Pioneer Batt.	A.B.B
	14		Went on leave	A.B.B
	28		Returned from leave.	A.B.B

AC Bowlby Maj
DADVS 29th Division

Army Form C. 2118.

WAR DIARY
or
INTELLIGENCE SUMMARY.
(Erase heading not required.)

DADVS
29th Division

Place	Date	Hour	Summary of Events and Information	Remarks and references to Appendices
	29/12/17		Inspected arrivals of Div H⁰ Qrs. - Signal Coy R.E. - Police	ABB
	30 -		Nothing to note	ABB
	31 -		Inspected arrivals of 87th Inf Bde + No 3 Coy Div train	ABB

H P Bowhay Maj
DADVS 29th Division

Army Form C. 2118.

WAR DIARY
or
INTELLIGENCE SUMMARY.
(Erase heading not required.)

DADVS 29th Division

Place	Date	Hour	Summary of Events and Information	Remarks and references to Appendices
Tincourt	1/4/18		Inspected 86th Inf Bde & HQ 2 Coy Div train	ADB
	2		Inspected 3rd Fd Coy R.E.	ADB
	3		Animals of 1/2 Monmouthshire Pioneer Batt & Div M.G. Coy.	ADB
	4		Moved to new area. Made out weekly returns re foot	ADB
	5		Inspected animals of 86th Inf Bde & HQ 3 Coy Div train	ADB
	6		Nothing to note	ADB
	7		Inspected animals of 17th Bde R.F.A.	ADB
	8		15" R.H.A.	ADB
	9		DAC & HQ 1 Coy Div train	ADB
	10		86th Inf Bde & HQ 2 Coy Div train	ADB
	11		Held a meeting of VO's of the Division. Made out weekly returns re foot.	ADB
	12		Attended conference at Office of ADVS 8th Corps.	ADB
	13		Inspected animals of Div H.Q. Signal Coy R.E. & Police	ADB
	14		" " of 87th Inf Bde & HQ 3 Coy Div train	ADB
	15		" " of 3rd Coy R.E. & Div M.G. Coy.	ADB
	16		" " of 88th Inf Bde & HQ 4 Coy Div train	ADB

ABBuckley Major
DADVS 29th Division

Army Form C. 2118.

WAR DIARY
or
INTELLIGENCE SUMMARY.

(Erase heading not required.)

DADVS 29th Division

Instructions regarding War Diaries and Intelligence Summaries are contained in F. S. Regs., Part II. and the Staff Manual respectively. Title pages will be prepared in manuscript.

Place	Date	Hour	Summary of Events and Information	Remarks and references to Appendices
	17/1/18		Visited Artillery lines	A.3.13
	18		Held a meeting of V.O's of the Division. Made out weekly returns & reports	A.3.13
	19		Moved to new area	A.3.13
	20		Inspected 17th Bde R.F.A.	A.3.13
	21		" animals of 87 Inf Bde	A.3.13
	22		" " of 86 " "	A.3.13
	23		" " of 1st Lancashire Fusiliers Bath. Div H.Q. Coy.	A.3.13
	24		Inspected animals of D.A.C.	A.3.5
	25		Held a meeting of V.O. of the Division. Made out weekly report returns	A.3.8
	26		Attended Conference at ADVS Office 8th Corps.	A.3.3
	27		Inspected animals of Div H.Q. Sqn, Signal Coy R.E. Police	A.3.13
	28		" " of 3rd Coy. R.E.	A.3.8
	29		" " of Div. Train	A.3.13
	30		" " of 86 Inf Bde.	A.3.8
	31		" " of 15th 13th Bttn R.H.N.	A.3.13

M.B. Bartley Maj
DADVS 29 Division

Army Form C. 2118.

WAR DIARY
or
INTELLIGENCE SUMMARY.
(Erase heading not required.)

DADVS 29th DIVISION Vol 8

Instructions regarding War Diaries and Intelligence Summaries are contained in F. S. Regs., Part II. and the Staff Manual respectively. Title pages will be prepared in manuscript.

Place	Date	Hour	Summary of Events and Information	Remarks and references to Appendices
	1/2/18		Held a meeting of V.O's. Made out weekly returns & reports	A/2/13
	2		Attended conference at ADVS office 8º Corps.	A/2/13
	3		Inspected animals of Div HdQrs Signal Coy RE & Police	A/3/13
	4		" 86th Bde Inf.	A/3/13
	5		" 17 Bde RFA	A/3/13
	6		" 87th Inf Bde	A/3/13
	7		D.A.C.	A/3/13
	8		Held a meeting of V.O's. made out weekly return reports. Inspected animals of 227 Div: h.t. Coy.	A/2/13
	9		Attended Conference at ADVS office 8º Corps	A/2/13
	10		Nothing to note.	A/2/13
	11		Inspected animals of 3 fd by RE.	A/2/13
	12		Moved to new Area.	A/2/13
	13		Inspected animals of 88th Inf Bde	A/2/13
	14		Div train	A/3/13

HBBowker Maj
DADVS 29 Division

Army Form C. 2118.

WAR DIARY
or
INTELLIGENCE SUMMARY.
(Erase heading not required.)

DADVS 29th Division

Place	Date	Hour	Summary of Events and Information	Remarks and references to Appendices
	15/2/18		Inspected Animals of 15th Bde R.H.A. Made out weekly returns reports.	A13.B
	16		Attended Conference at ADVS Office 8th Corps.	A13.B
			Inspected animals of Div H.Q. & Signal Coy R.E. Police	A13.B
	17		by 86th Inf Bde	P13.B
	18		87 "	P13.B
	19		29 M.G. Batt.	P13.B
	20		29 R.F.A.	P13.B
	21		17th Bde R.F.A.	P13.B
	22		Held meeting of V.O's of the Division. Made out weekly returns report.	P13.B
	23		Attended Conference at ADVS Office 8th Corps	P13.B
	24		North there.	
	25		Inspected animals of 37th Coy R.E.	P13.B
	26		Attended inspection of ADVS Corps of animals of 17th Bde R.F.A	W13.B
	27		Inspected animals of 10 Huss. Two which have just joined the Division	P13.B
	28		by DAPVS	P13.B

N.B. Bankay Maj
DADVS 29th Division

War Diary
of

Major A. B. Bowhay A.V.C.

D.A.D.V.S. 29th Division

From March 1.18   To March 31.18

Volume 9

Army Form C. 2118.

WAR DIARY
or
INTELLIGENCE SUMMARY.
(Erase heading not required.)

Volume 9

DADVS 29th Division

Instructions regarding War Diaries and Intelligence Summaries are contained in F. S. Regs., Part II. and the Staff Manual respectively. Title pages will be prepared in manuscript.

Place	Date	Hour	Summary of Events and Information	Remarks and references to Appendices
	March 1st 1918		Made out weekly returns & report for G.O.C. Inspected animals of 15th Bde R.H.A.	A.2.13.
	2		Attended Conference at ADVS office 8th Corps " " Div. Signal Coy R.E.	A.2.13.
	3		Nothing to note	A.2.13.
	4		Inspected 3 Field Coys R.E. animals	A.2.13.
	5		" " Ambulances animals	A.2.13.
	6		Visited sick lines of several units Inspected Div H.Q.W. horses	A.2.13.
	7		Inspected animals of two Inf Batts.	A.2.13.
	8		Moved with Division to a new area. Made out weekly returns. Report for G.O.C.	A.2.13.
	9		Attended Conference at ADVS office 8th Corps. Visited Artillery sick lines	A.2.13.
	10		Nothing to note	A.2.13.
	11		Inspected animals of 87th Inf Bde	A.2.13.
	12		" " 17th Bde R.F.A.	A.2.13.
	13		" " 88th Inf Bde	A.2.13.
	14		" " 1/2 Monmouth Pioneer Batt. & Div Signal Coy R.E.	A.2.13.
	15		Made out weekly returns, report for G.O.C.	A.2.13.

A.B. Bowlay
Maj. & Director
DADVS 29th Division

Army Form C. 2118.

WAR DIARY
or
INTELLIGENCE SUMMARY.
(Erase heading not required.)

D.A.D.V.S. 29th Division

Instructions regarding War Diaries and Intelligence Summaries are contained in F. S. Regs., Part II. and the Staff Manual respectively. Title pages will be prepared in manuscript.

Place	Date	Hour	Summary of Events and Information	Remarks and references to Appendices
	March 16.16		Attended conference at ADVS office 8th Corps – Inspected Div HQ horses	A.13.15
	17		Nothing to note	A.13.13
	18		Inspected animals of DAC	A.13.13
	19		" " of Div train ASC	A.13.13
	20		" " of 29th Batt MG Corps	A.13.13
	21		Attended conference held by DVS	A.13.13
	22		Made out weekly return report for GOC inspected animals of two Inf. Batt.	A.13.13
	23		Attended conference at ADVS office 8th Corps " " of Div HQ Ch: Div Signal Coy RE	A.13.13
	24		Member of a board on sheep Smiths.	A.13.13
	25		Inspected animals of 86th Inf Bde.	A.13.13
	26		" of Three field Ambulances	A.13.13
	27		" of Field Coys RE	A.13.13
	28		" of 88th Inf Bde	A.13.13
	29		" of 29th Batt MG Corps, 1/2 Monmouthshire Pioneer Batt. Made out weekly	A.13.13
	30		Attended conference at office of ADVS 8th Corps returns report for GOC	A.13.13
	31		Nothing to note	

A.B. Bowhay Maj.
D.A.D.V.S. 29th Division

War Diary of

Major. A. B. Bowlay. A.V.C.

D.A.D.V.S.

29th Division

From April 1.18   To April 30.18

Vol. X

Army Form C. 2118.

WAR DIARY
or
INTELLIGENCE SUMMARY.
(Erase heading not required.)

DADVS 29ᵈ Division

Place	Date	Hour	Summary of Events and Information	Remarks and references to Appendices
	1/4/16		Inspected animals of 15th Bde RHA	ARB
	2		" " " 17th Bde RFA	ARB
	3		" " " DAC	ARB
	4		" " " 87th Inf Bde.	ARB
	5		Made out weekly return report for G.O.C. Inspected animals of 1/2 Monmouth Pioneer Batt	ARB
	6		Attended conference at Offices of ADVS 6th Corps. Inspected animals of Div Signal Coy 29	ARB
	7		Nothing to note	ARB
	8		Inspected animals of 29 Div train	ARB
	9		Visited Artillery lines. Made arrangements with DADVS 41st Div to take over 29 Div stock were remaining in that area	ARB
	10		Moved from 6th Corps area to XV Corps area	ARB
	11		Moved Divisional area in XV Corps.	ARB
	12		Ditto. Made out weekly returns reports	ARB
	13		Visited office of ADVS XV Corps.	ARB
	14		Moved Divisional Area.	ARB
	15		Visited HQ of 2 Inf Bdes	ARB

AR Rowley Maj
DADVS 29ᵈ Division

Army Form C. 2118.

WAR DIARY
or
INTELLIGENCE SUMMARY.
(Erase heading not required.)

D.A.D.V.S. 29th Division

Instructions regarding War Diaries and Intelligence
Summaries are contained in F.S. Regs., Part II.
and the Staff Manual respectively. Title pages
will be prepared in manuscript.

Place	Date	Hour	Summary of Events and Information	Remarks and references to Appendices
	16/4/18		Inspected animals of SAA section DAC.	A.R.B.
	17/4/18		Inspected 3 Coys R.E.	A.R.B.
	18/4/18		Visited 2 DVH in another corps area. Took a new V.O. from this Division to 29 DA.	A.R.B.
	19/4/18		Moved to another area. Made out weekly returns report for G.O.C.	A.R.B.
	20/4/18		Inspected animals of 86th Inf Bde	A.R.B
	21/4/18		" " " " 87th Inf Bde.	A.R.B
	22/4/18		" " " " 88th Inf Bde.	A.R.B.
	23/4/18		Inspected animals of 1/2 Monmouth Pioneer Batt. & surplus Inf Batt transport	A.R.B.
	24/4/18		Inspected animals of an Inf Batt which has just joined the Div	A.R.B
	25/4/18		Made out weekly returns report for G.O.C. Inspected animals of the Signal Coy R.E.	A.R.B
	26/4/18		Inspected animals of Div HQrs.	A.R.B
	27/4/18		Nothing to note	A.R.B
	28/4/18		Moved to another area. Inspected animals of an Inf Batt which has just joined the Division	A.R.B.
	29/4/18		Moved to another area.	A.R.B
	30/4/18		Inspected animals of 3 Coys R.E.	A.R.B

A.R.Bowshay Maj.
D.A.D.V.S. 29th Division

War Diary /14
of

Major. A. B. Bawtray A.V.C
D.A.D.V.S. 29th Divn.

From May 1.18.   To May 31.18.

Vol. XI

Army Form C. 2118.

WAR DIARY
or
INTELLIGENCE SUMMARY. DADVS
(Erase heading not required.)

29 DIVISION

Vol XI

Instructions regarding War Diaries and Intelligence Summaries are contained in F. S. Regs., Part II. and the Staff Manual respectively. Title pages will be prepared in manuscript.

Place	Date	Hour	Summary of Events and Information	Remarks and references to Appendices
	1/5/18		Nothing to note - Ordinary routine work	A.B.B
	2		Inspected animals of 29" Battn F.G.C.B.	A.B.B
	3		Made out weekly returns report for Q.O.C.	A.B.B
	4		Nothing to note - Ordinary routine work	A.B.B
	5		"	A.B.B
	6		Inspected animals of 86" Inf. B.P.	A.B.B
	7		" 88 "	A.B.B
	8		" 87 "	A.B.B
	9		of K.O.S Heather R.F.	
	10		Made out weekly returns & report	A.B.B
	11		Inspected animals of Div. Signal Cy. R.E. & 1/2 Honewell Pioneer Batt.	A.B.B
	12		Nothing to note Ordinary routine work	A.B.B
	13		Attended ADVS on his inspection of animals of Div train & Squadron D.P.N	A.B.B
	14		Inspected animals of 3 Fd Coys R.E.	A.B.B
	15		Nothing to note - Ordinary routine work	A.B.B
	16		A member of a Board Examine Shoeing Smiths.	A.B.B

A7092 Wt.W1285.39/M1293 750,000. 1/17. D. D & L., Ltd. Forms/C2118/14.

Army Form C. 2118.

WAR DIARY
or
INTELLIGENCE SUMMARY. D.A.D.V.S. 29 DIVISION

(Erase heading not required.)

Instructions regarding War Diaries and Intelligence Summaries are contained in F. S. Regs., Part II. and the Staff Manual respectively. Title pages will be prepared in manuscript.

Place	Date	Hour	Summary of Events and Information	Remarks and references to Appendices
	17/5/18		A number of a Road Reasonne Shoein Smiths. Made out weekly returns & report	A.B.B.
	18/5/18		"	A.B.B.
	19/5/18		Nothing to note. Ordinary routine work	A.B.B.
	20/5/18		Attended A.D.V.S XV Corps on the inspection of animals of 15th Bde R.H.A	A.B.B.
	21/5/18		who had recently rejoined the Division	A.B.B.
	22/5/18		Inspected animals of DAC	A.B.B.
			" of 17th Bde RFA	A.B.B.
	23/5/18		Inspected animals of 86th Inf Bde	A.B.B.
	24		87 "	A.B.B.
	25		88 "	A.B.B.
	26		Nothing to note	A.B.B.
	27		Inspected 1/2 Movement Pervez Batt's animals	A.B.B.
	28		Nothing to note. Ordinary routine work	A.B.B.
	29		Inspected animals of 1/X th Middlesex Regt.	A.B.B.
	30		Inspected animals by 3 Coys R.E	A.B.B.
	31		Inspected animals of 29 Batt'n H.Q. Coys. Made out weekly returns & report	A.B.B.

D.A.D.V.S 29 Division

P.A. Bentley Major

War Diary
of

Major. A. B. Bowhay. A.V.C.
D.A.D.V.S. 29th Divn

From June.1.18. to June.30.18.

Volume. XII

DADVS
DADVS
29 Division
Vol 28

WAR DIARY
or
INTELLIGENCE SUMMARY.
(Erase heading not required.)

Army Form C. 2118.

Place	Date	Hour	Summary of Events and Information	Remarks and references to Appendices
	1/8/18		Nothing to note - ordinary routine work	A.B.B
	2/8/18		Nothing to note	A.B.B
	3/8/18		Inspected animals of 15th & 13th RFA	A.B.B
	4/8/18		" of 112 Bde RFA	A.B.B
	5		" of DAC	A.B.B
	6		" of 29 Batt MG Corps.	A.B.B
	7		Made out weekly returns reports	A.B.B
	8		Inspected animals of 3rd Coy R.E. Attended DDVS inspection 7/8 MVS	A.B.B
	9		Nothing to note.	A.B.B
	10		Inspected animals of 86th Inf Bde	A.B.B
	11		" 87 " "	A.B.B
	12		" 88 " "	A.B.B
	13		" 1/2 Monmouth Pioneer Batt.	A.B.B

A.B.Bowthorpe Major
DADVS 29th Div

WAR DIARY
or
INTELLIGENCE SUMMARY.

(Erase heading not required.)

Army Form C. 2118.

Instructions regarding War Diaries and Intelligence Summaries are contained in F. S. Regs., Part II. and the Staff Manual respectively. Title pages will be prepared in manuscript.

DADVS
29 Division

Place	Date	Hour	Summary of Events and Information	Remarks and references to Appendices
	14/6/18		Made out weekly returns report	A.2.3
	15/6/18		Inspected animals of XVI Middlesex Regt.	A.2.6
	16/6/18		Worken truck	A.2.3
	17/6/18		Inspected animals of Div: train A.S.C.	A.2.3 / A.2.3
	18/6/18		Inspected Div Signal Coy's animals	
	19/6/18		Worken truck	A.2.3
	20/6/18		Worken truck	M.2.3
	21/6/18		Made out weekly returns report. Attended conference at office of ADVS corps.	M.2.3
	22/6/18		Moved to a new area.	M.2.3
	23/6/18		Worken truck.	A.2.15
	24/6/18		Inspected animals of "g" Batt M.G.Coy.	M.2.15
	25/6/18		of 3rd Coy R.E.	M.2.3
	26/6/18		of 86" Inf Bde	A.2.15
	27		of 87 " "	M.2.0
	28		of 88 " Inf Bde. Made out weekly returns report	M.2.3
	29		of XVI Middlesex Regt.	M.2.15

W.B. Bowlby Major
DADVS 29 Division

War Diary
of
Major. A. B. Bowhay. A.V.C.
D.a.D.V.S.
29th Divn.

From July 1.18.   To July 31.18.

Volume X.

B.E.F.

Army Form C. 2118.

WAR DIARY
or
INTELLIGENCE SUMMARY.
(Erase heading not required.)

DADVS 29 DIVISION

Vol 2 /29

Place	Date	Hour	Summary of Events and Information	Remarks and references to Appendices
	1/7/18		Inspected animals of 15th Bde RHA	A.9.B
	2/7/18		" " " " 17th Bde RFA	A.2.8
	3/7/18		" " " " DAC	A.3.B
	4/7/18		" " " " 1/2 Monmouth Pioneer Batt	A.4.B
	5/7/18		Made out weekly returns + report	A.5.B
	6/7/18		Inspected animals of Div HQrs & Div Signal Coy RE	A.6.B
			No Thy Burke	A.7.B
	7/7/18		Inspected 3rd Fd Coy RE animals	
	8/7/18		attended 29 Divl Horse Show	A.8.B
	9/7/18		Inspected animals of 29 Div'n ham	A.9.B
	10/7/18		" " " " XVI Middlesex Reft	A.10.B
	11/7/18		Made out weekly return, reports	A.11.B
	12/7/18		Attended conference at HQrs officer	A.12.B
	13/7/18		No Thy Burke	A.13.B
	14/7/18		Inspected animals of 86 2nd Inf Bde	A.14.B
	15/7/18		" " " " 87 " " "	A.15.B
	16		" " " 88 " " "	
	17			

A.B. Bostock Maj
DADVS 29 Div.

Army Form C. 2118.

WAR DIARY
or
INTELLIGENCE SUMMARY.

(Erase heading not required.)

DADVS
29 DIVISION

Instructions regarding War Diaries and Intelligence Summaries are contained in F. S. Regs., Part II. and the Staff Manual respectively. Title pages will be prepared in manuscript.

Place	Date	Hour	Summary of Events and Information	Remarks and references to Appendices
	16/7/18		Visited sick lines of some artillery units & inspected 29 Field Amb. Coy animals	A.13.B
	19/7/18		Made out weekly return & report	A.13.B
	20/7/18		Inspected animals of Div. H.Q. & Div. Signal Coy R.E.	A.13.B
	21/7/18		Nothing to note	A.13.B
	22/7/18		Moved from XV Corps to X Corps area	A.13.B
	23/7/18		Moved over as in X Corps	A.13.B
	24/7/18		Inspected animals of 17 Bde R.F.A.	A.13.B
	25/7/18		Inspected animals by D.A.C.	A.13.B
	26/7/18		Made out weekly reports, returns & inspected animals of 1/1 Monmouth Reg.	A.13.B
	27/7/18		Inspected animals of 15-Bde R.H.A.	A.13.B
	28/7/18		Nothing to note	A.13.B
	29/7/18		Inspected animals of XVI Intelligence Dept. & Rein. to Coy R.E.	A.13.B
	30/7/18		Went on leave for 14 days U.K.	A.13.B

A.B.Bootle Maj. RAVC
DADVS 29 Div

War Diary
14 of
Major A. B. Bowhay. A.V.C.
D.A.D.V.S. 29 Divn

From Aug. 13. 18   To Aug. 31. 18.

Vol. XII

Vol. XII

WAR DIARY
or
INTELLIGENCE SUMMARY.

Army Form C. 2118.

DADVS 29 Division

Vol 30

Place	Date	Hour	Summary of Events and Information	Remarks and references to Appendices
	15/9/18		Returned from leave from U.K.	A13.B
	16/9/18		Ordinary routine work	A13.B
	17/9/18		Inspected animals of No.17 Bde R.F.A	A3.B
	18/9/18		Had out weekly returns reports. Inspected animals of 51st Inf Bde	A3.B
			Expected animals of 86 & Sup 13 Bde	A4.B
	17		nothing that	
	18		Inspected animals of 13 & Bde R.H.A	A3.B
	19		Ordinary Routine work	A4.B
	20		Inspected animals of 37th Army R.E.	A3.B
	21		" " 29 Bn D.L.I. M.G. Corps	A2.B
	22			A3.B
	23		Had weekly reports returns expected animals of 2nd H"Herts of 2 Squad 69.	A3.B
	24		Inspected animals of 31 Imps 28 + 1/2 howard Regt(Herts Bat)	A3.B
	25		nothing to report	A3.B

H.B. Bristley Mayor
SADVP 29 Divn

Army Form C. 2118.

WAR DIARY
or
INTELLIGENCE SUMMARY.
(Erase heading not required.)

DADVS 29th Division

Place	Date	Hour	Summary of Events and Information	Remarks and references to Appendices
	26/9/18		Inspected animals of XVI Middlesex Regt	A.818
	27		Visited some units lines	A.818
	28		Inspected Reserves of DAV	A.818
	29		" 29. Divisional train	A.818
	30		Visited horses & mules — Visited artillery sick lines	A.818
	31		Ordinary routine work.	A.818

A.B. Beesley
Major
DADVS 29 Division

War Diary   26
   of
Major. A. B. Bawtian A.D.C

D.a.D.V.S. 29 Division

From Sept. 1. 18   to   Sept. 30. 18.

Volume 15

Army Form C. 2118.

WAR DIARY
or
INTELLIGENCE SUMMARY.
(Erase heading not required.)

Volume 15   DADVS 29th Division

Instructions regarding War Diaries and Intelligence Summaries are contained in F.S. Regs., Part II. and the Staff Manual respectively. Title pages will be prepared in manuscript.

Place	Date	Hour	Summary of Events and Information	Remarks and references to Appendices
Wallon Cappel	1/9/18		Moved to Hazebrouck	A.B.13.
Hazebrouck	2/9/18		Visited 17th Bde R.F.A. wagon lines	A.B.13
"	3		" 86th Bde & Bath wagon lines	A.B.13
"	4		Made out weekly returns & reports.	A.B.B.
"	5		Visited 15th Bde R.H.A. wagon lines	A.B.13
"	6		Went forward to select position for 18 M.V.S.	A.B.13
"	7		Moved to Strazelle area	A.B.13
Strazelle	8		Visited 15th Bde R.H.A. wagon lines & see 34 cases of mustard oil gas blisters	A.B.13
"	9		Inspected 87 & Bde animals	A.B.13
"	10		Inspected 3 Pol Coys R.E. animals	A.B.13
"	11		Made out weekly returns reports. Took over charge from ADVS XV Corps while he went on leave.	A.B.B
"	12		Moved to Hazebrouck.	A.B.13
"	13		Nothing to note	A.B.13
"	14		Inspected 86th Bde animals	A.B.13
"	15		86th Bde animals & 1/2 Monmouth Pioneer Batt. animals	A.B.13.
"	16		Both H.Q. Corps animals. Handed over temporary duty of ADVS Corps as he returned, moved to II Corps	A.B.13
Vogeltje	17		Moved to II Corps area.	A.B.13

A.B. Brothey Maj
DADVS 29th Division

Army Form C. 2118.

WAR DIARY
or
INTELLIGENCE SUMMARY.
(Erase heading not required.)

DADVS
29 DIVISION

Instructions regarding War Diaries and Intelligence Summaries are contained in F. S. Regs., Part II. and the Staff Manual respectively. Title pages will be prepared in manuscript.

Place	Date	Hour	Summary of Events and Information	Remarks and references to Appendices
Vaqueze	18/9/18		Reported to ADVS 11 Corps. Made out weekly return report.	A.D.B.
	19/9/18		Inspected 29 Div Signal Coy. animals.	A.B.B
	20		Nothing doing.	A.B.B
	21		Inspected animals of Div HQ Coh & M.M.P.	A.B.B
	22		Inspected animals of D.A.C. & xvi Middlesex Regt.	A.B.B
	23		Inspected animals of 147 Bde R.F.A. attended conference at ADVS Office	A.B.B
	24		15 " Bde R.H.A.	A.B.B
	25		Made out weekly returns report.	A.B.B
	26		Visited a new area selected S.Depot 18 M.V.S.	A.B.B
	27		Moved to a new area.	A.B.B
Brake Camp	28		Inspected animals of 3 Fd ambulances.	A.B.B
	29		Visit pack animals in forward area.	A.B.B
	30		Visited transport lines of 3 Inf Bde.	A.B.B
	31		Selected site for 18 M.V.S in forward area.	A.B.B

H.A.Bouskey Maj
DADVS 29 Division

War Diary
of

Major A.B. Bowlay A.V.C
D.a.D.V.S. 29 Division

From Oct 1. 18.   To Oct 31. 18.

Volume No 16.

Army Form C. 2118.

WAR DIARY
or
INTELLIGENCE SUMMARY.
(Erase heading not required.)

DADVS 29 Division

Instructions regarding War Diaries and Intelligence Summaries are contained in F. S. Regs., Part II. and the Staff Manual respectively. Title pages will be prepared in manuscript.

Place	Date	Hour	Summary of Events and Information	Remarks and references to Appendices
	1/10/18		Inspected animals of the H. Corps R.E.	A.13.18
			88. Inf. Bde.	A.13.18
	2/10/18			A.13.18
	3/10/18		Moved to another area.	A.13.18
	4/10/18		Made out weekly return report. Inspected animals 706² Inf. Bde.	A.13.18
	5/10/18		Moved to another area	A.13.18
	6/10/18		Visited R-Artillery units sick lines	A.13.18
	7/10/18		Inspected animals of 87² Inf. Bde.	A.13.18
	8/10/18		Moved to another area	A.13.18
				A.13.18
	9/10/18		Inspected animals of 29 Batt. M.G. Corps	A.13.18
	10/10/18		Inspected animals of 3 Coys of R.E.	A.13.18
	11/10/18		Made out weekly report. Inspected animals of 1/2 Honourable Persian Batt.	A.13.18
	12/10/18		Inspected 29 Div Signal Coy animals & Horses of M.M.P.	A.13.18
	13/10/18		Selected site for Adv M.V.S. & for 110 M.V.S.	A.13.18
	14/10/18		Visited sick lines of Inf. units	A.13.18
	15/10/18		S.B. & I. site for Adv. & Div. advanced pool	A.13.18
	16/10/18		Moved to future area	A.13.18
	17/10/18		Inspected animals of 1/2 Lt. Ambulances + XVI Huddersley Regt.	A.13.18
	18/10/18		Made out weekly report. Inspected site for M.V.S. + adv. pool.	A.13.18
	19/10/18		Visited Artillery units sick lines.	A.13.18

J. A. Brisley Major
DADVS 29 Div.

Army Form C. 2118.

WAR DIARY
or
INTELLIGENCE SUMMARY.

D.A.D.V.S. 29 Division

(Erase heading not required.)

Instructions regarding War Diaries and Intelligence Summaries are contained in F. S. Regs., Part II. and the Staff Manual respectively. Title pages will be prepared in manuscript.

Place	Date	Hour	Summary of Events and Information	Remarks and references to Appendices
	20/10/16		Moved to new area.	A/3/B
	21/10/16		Selected site for 18 M.V.S.	A/3/B
	22/10/16		Inspect 2 animals of D.H.Q.	A/3/B
	23/10/16		Inspected " " 13th R.H.A	A/3/12
	24/10/16		" " " B" 86 R.F.A.	A/3/4
	25/10/16		" " " B" 11 86 R.F.A.	A/3/B
			Made out weekly reports + returns	
	26/10/16		Nothing to note	
	27/10/16		Moved from " Corps to XV Corps area	A/3/B
	28/10/16		Inspected Animals of 3 76 Coys R.E.	A/3/B
	29/10/16		Inspected animals Hd.Qs. 87 Inf Bde, 7/0 + Ken's Bty Train	A/3/B
	30/10/16		Inspect animals of B Wheelwright	A/3/B
	31/10/16		Inspect 87 & 88 coys 13 de. 86 11 Bty train & 85 & 89 ambulances	A/3/B

M.A. Barker Maj
D.A.D.V.S. 29 Dvn 31/10/16

War Diary
of
A.A.D.M.S. 29 Division

From 1/11/18   To 30/11/18.

Vol. 17

Vol. IV. No. 81.

Army Form C. 2118.

DADVS 29th Division

WAR DIARY
or
INTELLIGENCE SUMMARY.
(Erase heading not required.)

No. 34

Place	Date	Hour	Summary of Events and Information	Remarks and references to Appendices
	1/11/18		Made out weekly returns report. Inspected animals of 87th Inf. Bn. & about two fd Bdy of R.E.	A.B.B
	2/11/18		Attended conference at ADVS office 15 Corps.	A.B.B
	3/11/18		Nothing to note	A.B.B
	4/11/18		Inspected animals of 29 'B' Batt'n Q. Corps.	A.B.B
	5/11/18		" 86th Inf Bde - a fd amb. & a Coy of R.E	A.B.B
	6/11/18		" of 15th 2nd Bde R.H.A.	A.B.B
	7/11/18		Left XV Corps area for 2 Corps	A.B.B
	8/11/18		Made out weekly returns report. - Visited ADVS office reported arrival	A.B.B
	9/11/18		Inspected animals of D.A.C	A.B.B
	10/11/18		Nothing to note	A.B.B
	11/11/18		Moved areas.	A.B.B
	12/11/18		Inspected animals of 17th Bde R.F.A.	A.B.B
	13/11/18		Moved areas.	A.B.B
	14/11/18		Ditto	A.B.B
	15/11/18		Changed from 10 Corps to 2 Corps. Inspected animals 88th Inf Bn. Div Hd Ab.	A.B.B
	16/11/18		Made out weekly report returns - Inspected animals of Div Signals Div Hd Ab.	A.B.B
	17/11/18		Inspected animals of 2 Corps Div train & a fd amb.	A.B.B

A.R. Brokeshay Maj
DADVS 29 Div.

Army Form C. 2118.

WAR DIARY
or
INTELLIGENCE SUMMARY.
(Erase heading not required.)

DADVS 29 Division

Instructions regarding War Diaries and Intelligence Summaries are contained in F. S. Regs., Part II. and the Staff Manual respectively. Title pages will be prepared in manuscript.

Place	Date	Hour	Summary of Events and Information	Remarks and references to Appendices
	18/10/18		Moved to other area. Inspected by transport on the march	ADVS
	19/10/18		Nothing to note.	ADVS
	20/10/18		Visited Artillery sick lines	ADVS
	21/10/18		Moved to other area. Inspected Artillery animals on the march	ADVS
	22/10/18		Made out weekly returns report.	ADVS
	23/10/18		Moved to other area. Inspected animals of 2 Bde Group on the march	ADVS
	24/10/18		Moved to other area.	ADVS
	25/10/18		Ditto — Inspected animals of A.B.[?] Group on the march.	ADVS
	26/10/18		Nothing to note.	ADVS
	27/10/18		Moved to other area. Inspected animals of 3rd Bde Group on the march.	ADVS
	28/10/18		Moved to other area.	ADVS
	29/10/18		Made out weekly returns reports.	ADVS
	30/10/18		Moved to other area.	ADVS

AM Rowley Maj.
DADVS 29 Division

War Diary

of

Major. A.B. Bowhay. R.A.V.C.
D.A.D.V.S.
29 Division.

From. 1/12/18. To 31/12/18.

Army Form C. 2118.

WAR DIARY
or
INTELLIGENCE SUMMARY.

DADVS 29 Division

Vol 35

(Erase heading not required.)

Place	Date	Hour	Summary of Events and Information	Remarks and references to Appendices
	1/12/18		Moved to another area.	A28
	2/12/18		Moved to another area. Inspected animals of Div Artillery on the march.	A28
	3/12/18		Visited sick lines of some units.	A28
	4/12/18		Moved to another area. Inspected animals of a Bde group on the march.	A28
	5/12/18		Moved to another area.	A28
	6/12/18		Moved to another area. Made out weekly returns, reports	A28
	7/12/18		Moved to another area. Inspected animals of a Bde group on the march.	A28
	8/12/18		Nothing to note.	A28
	9/12/18		Moved to another area. Inspected animals of a Bde group on the march.	A28
	10/12/18		Visited sick lines of some units.	A28
	11/12/18		Visited ADVS office	A28
	12/12/18		Visited sick lines of some units	A28
	13/12/18		Moved to another area. Made out weekly returns, report	A28
	14/12/18		Nothing to note	A28
	15/12/18		Nothing to note	~~A28~~
	16/12/18		Visited sick lines of some units.	A28

A.B. Bradley
Major
DADVS 29 Division

Army Form C. 2118.

WAR DIARY
or
INTELLIGENCE SUMMARY.

(Erase heading not required.)

DADVS
29th Division

Instructions regarding War Diaries and Intelligence Summaries are contained in F. S. Regs., Part II. and the Staff Manual respectively. Title pages will be prepared in manuscript.

Place	Date	Hour	Summary of Events and Information	Remarks and references to Appendices
	17/12/15		Nothing to note.	A.R.B.
	18/12/15		Nothing to note.	A.R.B.
	19/12/15		Nothing to note.	A.R.B.
	20/12/15		Made out weekly report returns.	A.R.B.
	21/12/15		Moved to another area.	A.R.B.
	22/12/15		Nothing to note.	A.R.B.
	23/12/15		Inspected animals of 17th Bde R.F.A.	A.R.B.
	24/12/15		Moved to another area.	A.R.B.
	25/12/15		Inspected animals of D.M.C.	A.R.B.
	26/12/15		Inspected animals of two coys of the Div. train.	A.R.B.
	27/12/15		Made out weekly return report.	A.R.B.
	28/12/15		Inspected animals of 86th Inf Bde.	A.R.B.
	29/12/15		Nothing to note.	A.R.B.
	30/12/15		Inspected animals of 29th Div Signals & 15th Bde R.H.A.	A.R.B.
	31/12/15		"	A.R.B.

A.B.Rowlay
Major
DADVS 29 Division

**RHINE ARMY
SOUTHERN DIVISION
LATE 29TH DIVISION**

DEP. ASST DIR. VETERINARY SERVICES

JAN - OCT 1919

2070 / 2084

War Diary
of

Major. A. B. Bowkay R.A.V.C.
D.A.D.V.S.
29 Division

from Jan. 1. 19 to Jan. 31. 19.
Volume. 19

WAR DIARY
or
INTELLIGENCE SUMMARY.
(Erase heading not required.)

Army Form C. 2118.

DADVS
29ᵈ Division

Instructions regarding War Diaries and Intelligence Summaries are contained in F.S. Regs., Part II. and the Staff Manual respectively. Title pages will be prepared in manuscript.

Place	Date	Hour	Summary of Events and Information	Remarks and references to Appendices
Germany	1/1/19		Nothing to note.	
	2/1/19		Inspected animals of 76 & 2 Inf Bde & 3 Fd Coys R.E.	ADB. ODB.
	3		Office reclassification of all animals in the Division	ARB
			Visited ADVS office & 1st Station D.H.C. DH & A Cb.	HBB
	4		Classified all animals of 1st Station D.H.C. No 1 Coy Dn train	ARB
	5		" " No 3 Section D.H.C.	
	6		" " No 2 "	
			" 89 Fd ambulance Essex Yeomanry &	
			Royal Fusiliers & No 2 Coy Dn train	ARB
	7		Classified animals of 3 Batteries of 147 Bde. B & D H Q Cb. 29 Div H Q Cb, 87 Fd ambulance	ARB
			& No 3 Coy Div train	
	8		" " of 86ᵗʰ Inf Bde. HQ & 4 Coy Div train. & 3 Batteries.	ARB
	9		" " of 15 Bde HQ Cb & 3 Batteries.	ARB
	10		" " 3 Fd Coys R.E. & 67 Fd Bde	ARB
	11		" " 29th Batt ng Corps - Div train H Q Cb, Div Signal Coy	ARB
	12		" " 18 M.V.S. XVI Middlesex Regt DA H & Q Cb. HQ Cb 86 Inf Bde	ARB
	13		" " L Batt of 15ᵗʰ Bde & ½ Monmouth Regt, Div Police	ARB
	14		" " 2 Batteries 36ᵈ Bde & 86 2 Fd Amb.	ARB
	15		" " & Ammunition Column.	ARB

H.B.Berkeley Major
DADVS 29ᵗʰ Division

WAR DIARY
or
INTELLIGENCE SUMMARY.
(Erase heading not required.)

Army Form C. 2118.

DADVS DADVS 29th DIVISION.

Place	Date	Hour	Summary of Events and Information	Remarks and references to Appendices
Germany	16/1/19		Changed arrival of D17 Bat 19th Btn & R Dub Fusiliers	A.B.B
	17/1/19		Ordinary Routine work.	A.B.B
	18		"	A.B.B
	19		Nothing to note.	A.B.B
	20		Ordinary Routine work.	A.B.B.
	21		Changed arrival of J cable section att. to 29 Div. Signals	A.B.B
	22		Ordinary Routine work.	A.B.B.
	23		"	A.B.B.
	24		"	A.B.B.
	25		"	A.B.B
	26		Nothing to note.	A.B.B
	27		Ordinary Routine work.	A.B.B
	28		"	A.B.B
	29		"	A.B.B
	30		"	A.B.B
	31		"	A.B.B

A.M Bookey Major
DADVS 29th Division

War Diary 22
of
Capt. A.B. Bowlay R.A.V.C.
D.a.D.V.S. 29 Division

From Feb.1.1919   To Feb.28.1919

Volume No 20.

D.A.D.V.S.,
29TH
DIVISION.
No. 16/1
Date. 1/3/19.

Vol. No 20

WAR DIARY
or
INTELLIGENCE SUMMARY.
(Erase heading not required)

Army Form C. 2118.

DADVS
29 Division

Vol 37

Place	Date	Hour	Summary of Events and Information	Remarks and references to Appendices
January 1/2/19	1		Disinfected animals of 1st Bdy Group the Battn of Bn trans	#15/1
	2		Visiting Depots	#2
	3		Inspected animals for Remits	#3
	4		" "	#4
	5		" 15 RFA	#5
	6		Inspected animals of Windsor Hill Div Royal Engrs	#6
			" 29 Battn E. Corps	#7
	8		Visiting Depots	
	9		Visiting Depots	#10
	10		Inspected animals of 87 & 88 Bde Group	#11
	11		" 86 Bde Group	#12
	12		Visiting Depots	
	13		Examined animals with Lt Col Russell Wood	#13/S
	14		ditto	#14
	15		ditto	#15

Army Form C. 2118.

WAR DIARY
or
INTELLIGENCE SUMMARY.
(Erase heading not required.)

Instructions regarding War Diaries and Intelligence Summaries are contained in F. S. Regs., Part II. and the Staff Manual respectively. Title pages will be prepared in manuscript.

Place	Date	Hour	Summary of Events and Information	Remarks and references to Appendices
Germany	16/2/19			
	17			
	18			
	19			
	20			
	21			
	22			
	23			
	24			
	25			
	26			
	27			
	28			

Army Form C. 2118.

WAR DIARY
or
INTELLIGENCE SUMMARY.
(Erase heading not required.)

D.A.D.V.S. SOUTHERN DIVISION

Instructions regarding War Diaries and Intelligence Summaries are contained in F. S. Regs., Part II. and the Staff Manual respectively. Title pages will be prepared in manuscript.

Place	Date	Hour	Summary of Events and Information	Remarks and references to Appendices
Germany	1/5/19		Ordinary Routine work	A.D.B
	2		"	A.D.B
	3		"	A.D.B
	4		"	A.D.B
	5		"	A.D.B
	6		"	A.D.B
	7		"	A.D.B
	8		"	A.D.B
	9		"	A.D.B
	10		"	A.D.B
	12		"	A.D.B
	13		"	A.D.B
	14		"	A.D.B
	15		"	A.D.B
	16		"	A.D.B
	17		"	A.D.B
	18		"	A.D.B
	19		"	A.D.B
	20		"	A.D.B
	21		"	A.D.B
	22		"	A.D.B
	23		"	A.D.B
	24		"	A.D.B
	25		"	A.D.B
	26		"	A.D.B
	27		"	A.D.B
	28		"	A.D.B
	29		"	A.D.B
	30		"	A.D.B
	31		"	A.D.B

H.R.Bowtly Major
D.A.D.V.S. Southern Division

War Diary
of

Major A.B. Barclay DaD.A.S.
5th Division.
For month ending 30 June 19.

Volume No. 24.

KMc

Volume No 24

Army Form C. 2118.

WAR DIARY
or
INTELLIGENCE SUMMARY.
(Erase heading not required.)

D.A.D.V.S.
SOUTHERN DIVISION.

Instructions regarding War Diaries and Intelligence Summaries are contained in F. S. Regs., Part II. and the Staff Manual respectively. Title pages will be prepared in manuscript.

Place	Date	Hour	Summary of Events and Information	Remarks and references to Appendices
Germany	1/6/17 to 29/6/17		Nothing to note - ordinary routine work.	A.R.B.
	30/6/17		Departed for 14 days leave to U.K.	A.R.B.

A.B Bowlby Major
D.A.D.V.S. Southern Division

WAR DIARY
or
INTELLIGENCE SUMMARY.
(Erase heading not required.)

Army Form C. 2118.

D.A.D.V.S. Southern Division

Place	Date	Hour	Summary of Events and Information	Remarks and references to Appendices
Germany	1/7/19 to 14/7/19		On leave U.K.	A.B.B.
	15/7/19		Joined Division from leave.	A.B.B.
	16/7/19		A member of Board for classification of animals in the Division	A.B.B.
	17/7/19		Ditto	A.B.B.
	18/7/19		"	A.B.B.
	19/7/19		Nothing to note.	A.B.B.
	20/7/19		A member of Board for classification of animals in the Division	A.B.B.
	21/7/19			A.B.B.
	22/7/19 to 31/7/19		Ordinary Routine work.	A.B.B.

A.B. Bowley Major
D.A.D.V.S. Southern Division

War Diary
of
Major A.B. Bowhay R.A.V.C
D.a.D.V.S.
Southern Division

from 1/8/19 to 29/8/19

Volume No 26.

//June No 6

WAR DIARY
or
INTELLIGENCE SUMMARY.

Army Form C. 2118.

D A D V S
Southern Division

(Erase heading not required.)

Place	Date	Hour	Summary of Events and Information	Remarks and references to Appendices
Germany	1/8/19. to 21/8/19		Ordinary Routine work. Nothing to note.	ARB
	22/8/19.		Attended inspection of 1st M.V.S. by D.V.S. Rhine Army	ARB
	23/8/19 to 28/8/19		Ordinary Routine work.	ARB
	29/8/19		Handed over to Capt. J. Edgar R.A.V.C. Proceeded to the Midlands	ARB
			Division on D.A.D.V.S.	

H B Bowlay Major
D A D V S
Southern Division

Army Form C. 2118.

2 a DVS

WAR DIARY
or
INTELLIGENCE SUMMARY.
(Erase heading not required.)

Instructions regarding War Diaries and Intelligence Summaries are contained in F. S. Regs, Part II. and the Staff Manual respectively. Title pages will be prepared in manuscript.

Place	Date	Hour	Summary of Events and Information	Remarks and references to Appendices
Berg Gladbach	1/9/19		Took over duties SADVS. Northern Division.	
"	2/9/19		Inspected 18th M.V.S.	
"	3/9/19		Inspected animals of 113th Bde R.F.A. with ADVS. II Corps	
"	4/9/19		" " 96th Bde RFA	
"	5/9/19		" " 10th Inf. Bde.	
"	6/9/19		" " 3rd Inf. Bde.	
"	7/9/19		Ot bank. 6 U.K.	
"	22/9/19		Inspected 18 M.V.S. & Machine Gun Battn.	
"	23/9/19		Inspected. 2 ad Inf Bde.	
"	24/9/19		" 9 & Gloucesters & M.V.S.	
"	25/9/19		" 6 d Field Ambulance	

1577 Wt. W10/91/1773 500,000 5/15 D D & L A.D.S.S./Forms/C. 2118.

Army Form C. 2118.

WAR DIARY
or
INTELLIGENCE SUMMARY.
(Erase heading not required.)

Instructions regarding War Diaries and Intelligence Summaries are contained in F.S. Regs., Part II. and the Staff Manual respectively. Title pages will be prepared in manuscript.

Place	Date	Hour	Summary of Events and Information	Remarks and references to Appendices
Berg Gladbach	27/9/19		Visited S.A.C.	
"	28/9/19		Visited S.R.S. 10th & 12th Cyc. Train	
"	29/9/19		Visited M.V.S. Signal Coy. & Hd. Qr. Train	
"	30/9/19		" 113 I. Bde. H.Q.	

W. M. St. H. Rue
Lt.Col. S. Saxton Brown

WAR DIARY
or
INTELLIGENCE SUMMARY.
(Erase heading not required)

Army Form C. 2118.

Southern Div

Place	Date	Hour	Summary of Events and Information	Remarks and references to Appendices
Berg Gladbach	1/10/19		Visited 126 L Bde B'P'A, LdR A.D.V.S. & C/Ps.	
	2/10/19		" 2 st. Iy Bde 10th " " "	
	3/10/19		" 1+2 Sections S.A.C. M.V.S.	
	4/10/19		" 9 Gloucesters. evacuated 6 animals	
	27/9/19		" 18th M.V.S.	
	8/10/19		Inspected all instruments at M.V.S.	
			Inspected animals for evacuation from M.V.S. (6 b Hb 2 V.E.S)	
Wur	7/10/19		Visited 88th Field Ambulance evacuated 4 animals for sale.	
	8/10/19		Inspected animals for evacuation from M.V.S. Visited 1st Bde HQ	
			Inspected Signal Coy. Evacuated 1 D.L.E.S. 2 Vees (N.b.)	

Army Form C. 2118.

WAR DIARY
or
INTELLIGENCE SUMMARY.
(Erase heading not required.)

Place	Date	Hour	Summary of Events and Information	Remarks and references to Appendices
Berg en Alsebeck	9/10/19		Inspected animals for Observation from M.V.S.	
	10/10/19		Inspected animals for Retention in Veterinary Section in Hospital one. No 1. 2. 3 Sections one.	
	16/10/19		Inspected animals for retention in Veterinary Section in 2/M.G. Battn. H.Q. 2nd Inf. Bde. 32nd Bearer. D Bty. 113 Bde + Signal Coy.	
	11/10/19		Inspected animals for retention in. 113th Bde RFA.	
	12/10/19		" " " " M.M.P. DHQ. + CBdy. 110 Bde.	
	13/10/19		" " " " 178 L Bde RFA.	
	14/10/19		Visited B.A. HQ + interview with Col Brown. S.V.O. II Div. asking leave for Relaxation of Closing down for Relaxation.	

Army Form C. 2118.

WAR DIARY
or
INTELLIGENCE SUMMARY.
(Erase heading not required.)

Instructions regarding War Diaries and Intelligence Summaries are contained in F. S. Regs., Part II. and the Staff Manual respectively. Title pages will be prepared in manuscript.

Place	Date	Hour	Summary of Events and Information	Remarks and references to Appendices
Berg Gladbach				
	15/10/19		Visited Pr. Offizieren Genesen Abteilung Home for returnees	
	16/10/19		" " "	
	17/10/19		A.D.M.S. visited M.V.S. Inspected Crumbs for Evacuation	
	18/10/19		Visited 87 Field Ambulance. Inspected Crumbs as Scheme for Retention	
	19/10/19		Visited M.V.S. D.D.M.S. evacuated Offiziere Case	
	20/10/19		Visited M.V.S. No 3 Sabin Bal. & 88th Field Ambulance	
	21/10/19		Visited M.V.S. H.Q. 1st Inf. Bde. & H.Q. Divisional Train	
	22/10/19		Visited M.V.S. 57 Warwick & Nor Coy. Train	

Army Form C. 2118.

WAR DIARY
or
INTELLIGENCE SUMMARY.
(Erase heading not required)

Instructions regarding War Diaries and Intelligence Summaries are contained in F. S. Regs., Part II. and the Staff Manual respectively. Title pages will be prepared in manuscript.

Place	Date	Hour	Summary of Events and Information	Remarks and references to Appendices
Bergehnbach	23/10/19		Visited M.V.S. Not last one. t/o German.	
	24/10/19		ADMS visited M.V.S. Re party of personnel visited HQ copy Res	
	25/10/19		Visited Capt. Burns inspected annex for for retention	
			Q of Gloucesters	
	26/10/19		Visited Loreau Division Train Kill RE. Train to Billet ann. E. Armentin	
	27/10/19		Visited M.V.S. & DDMS	
	28/10/19		Visited Hrs. Cy. No 3 + 4 Cy. & M.V.S.	
	28/10/19		Visited M.V.S. H8 4 Field Ambulance. Fourth Section one. arranged	
			for them to attend	
	29/10/19		Brought up Division.	
			For Independent Statement to HQs. Long C.	

Army Form C. 2118.

WAR DIARY
or
INTELLIGENCE SUMMARY.
(Erase heading not required.)

Instructions regarding War Diaries and Intelligence Summaries are contained in F. S. Regs., Part II. and the Staff Manual respectively. Title pages will be prepared in manuscript.

Place	Date	Hour	Summary of Events and Information	Remarks and references to Appendices
Boulogne	30/6/19		Visited M.H.S. Bry & Ambulance Trains for Evening trains	
	31/6/19		Visited Ambulance R.T.O. Inspecting animals for relation	

www.ingramcontent.com/pod-product-compliance
Lightning Source LLC
Chambersburg PA
CBHW081532160426
43191CB00011B/1745